A SOLUTION-FOCUSED CULTURE

FROM REGULATION TO RESOURCE

TIM BOLDUC

JESSICA LEAVINS

SFC ENTERPRISE

PRAISE FOR A SOLUTION FOCUSED CULTURE

"In uncertain times, more than ever, we need our communities to be a source of stability and strength. That requires local governments that are aligned, engaged, and focused on serving citizens. This book shows us what building such a culture looks like in action. It's the perfect mix of good storytelling (to pull readers in and make them want to learn) and tactical advice (to help them apply the lessons to their own local government). Thank you, Tim and Jessica, for creating a teaching tool for all citizens, public and private, who want local governments that get things done as they work for the good of everyone."

-Quint Studer
Founder, Educator, Philanthropist
Author of Building a Vibrant Community

"Written in the story-tale style of the 1988 classic, 'Zapp! The Human Lightning of Empowerment' by Byham and Cox, 'A Solution-Focused Culture' provides a peek behind the curtain for leaders who want to shift culture and empower followers."

-Dr. joyce gillie gossom
Organizational & Leadership Consultant
Author of *Why Are They Following Me?*

"I personally admire Tim Bolduc's leadership in my hometown, as he is uniquely adept in the approach of building trust and culture as an effective means for serving the public and solving community challenges! Tim and Jessica are making a tremendous impact in our community as they implement a Solution Focused Culture. "

-Paul Hsu Ph.D
Founder, engineer, entrepreneur, and public servant.
Author of *Guardians of the Dream*

FOREWORD

One of my biggest passions is helping communities become the best they can be. And because I've had the good fortune of working with Tim Bolduc, I know he shares this passion.

I was fortunate to meet Tim some years back when I was helping the city of Fort Walton Beach, Florida, create a strategic implementation plan. Tim impressed me with his skill in understanding complexity and quickly prioritizing the actions needed to achieve great outcomes. When he called me to discuss the Crestview opportunity, I was excited for him and the community. It was no surprise that Tim quickly created a "get it done" culture. His business background led to a culture of working together to serve citizens and build up the community.

Tim is supersmart. He knows his stuff. When looking to revitalize a community, mastering skills like policy management and contract negotiation is important. You also need to be a visionary thinker, an engaged citizen, a natural connector, and a tribe builder. That's what it takes to move past the "great idea" phase and get people inspired, engaged, and ready to move past their natural resistance and act. Tim has all these qualities.

FOREWORD

I was excited when he shared with me that he and his colleague Jessica Leavins were writing a book on culture change in city government. While it's important to have the right person in a leadership position, the entire team needs to be aligned, enthusiastic, and focused on the right things. How else will they convince the community to move forward?

One thing that makes *A Solution-Focused Culture* impactful is that it's part fable and part technical application. After you've been inspired by the story of TJ and the city of Clearview, you get the step-by-step blueprint for changing the culture of your own organization. It's the best of both worlds.

I've always believed in the power of stories. Facts and data alone don't change behavior; storytelling does. It grabs readers, pulls them in, and touches them on an emotional level. It moves minds and hearts. Because the information in this book is presented as a story, citizens are more likely to want to read it. The more people know, the better citizens they become. Educating and engaging them is the most powerful tool we have in bringing change to communities.

Nowhere have I seen this truth play out more clearly than in the impact of Pensacola's own CivicCon series. We created CivicCon, which is short for "civic conversations," to educate all citizens. By bringing in community-building experts from different areas of government and private industry, we have been able to raise civic IQ and build a lot of trust. The more people understand the revitalization process and see how different sectors can come together to make life better for everyone, the more likely they are to feel good about growth initiatives.

I think of this book the same way. It's a wonderful tool for educating and building trust.

The story format also helps to showcase what it's like to work in city government. That makes it so valuable to citizens, business leaders, and those in other sectors like healthcare, education, and nonprofit. Sometimes we make assumptions about how things operate. When we understand what others' lives are like, it can shift how we engage with them. This includes citizens.

A Solution-Focused Culture is a great book for many audiences. I recommend it for:

- Government leaders who want to strengthen the culture in their own organization.
- Managers and frontline employees. The book can serve as a helpful training tool, study guide, and resource they can refer to again and again.
- Business leaders and others who have a stake in revitalizing communities. The story humanizes local government and helps people see them as partners, not adversaries.
- Students and young people who might be interested in a career in city government.
- Community members and anyone and everyone who wants to know more about what proactive, positive, customer-centric public service looks like in action.

We all have a stake in making our communities stronger, better, and more sustainable. In the face of disruption and chaos, *home* should be a place that offers stability and shelter from the storm. The more informed and educated we are about how local government works, the more likely we are to be able to create such places.

Thank you, Tim and Jessica, for showing what an agile and innovative city government culture can look like—one that puts citizens first and sets their community up to thrive.

—Quint Studer
Author of *Building a Vibrant Community: How Citizen-Powered Change Is Reshaping America*

INTRODUCTION

A Solution-Focused Culture was co-authored by a city manager with over thirty years of experience leading organizations, starting in the private sector and eventually local government, and a Human Resources director with over ten years of experience working in the public sector. This book was born from countless conversations we had about the challenges facing local governments, particularly regarding culture, efficiency, and leadership. We've seen first-hand how small, tight-knit organizations like city governments can get bogged down in unnecessary bureaucracy and how it takes real leadership—not just management—to turn things around.

The characters in this book are not meant to represent any real individuals. Rather, they are a reflection of the collective experiences we've had working for and with local governments across the country. The truth is that the vast majority of people who work in government are honest, hard-working individuals who truly want to serve their communities and do the right thing. Unfortunately, what often happens, particularly in small governments, is that the organization fails its employees. It fails them by not providing

INTRODUCTION

opportunities for growth through leadership training, by promoting based on tenure or technical skills alone, and by undervaluing education and technology due to budget constraints.

Too often, we see employees promoted into management roles simply because they have years of experience or excel at the technical side of their job. While these factors are essential, they often create managers who focus on processes rather than leaders who inspire change. Without proper leadership training, these managers tend to fall back on what they know best—the technical aspects of the job—and this frequently leads to an increase in bureaucracy. They add more paperwork, more steps, and more regulation instead of addressing the root of the issue. This is a widespread problem in government.

We see this tendency in the clerk who rejects a form because a box wasn't checked or the supervisor who creates more paperwork to address a symptom without looking at the source of the problem. It's not the fault of the individual; it's often the organization that has failed them. The organization fails when it doesn't give employees the freedom to pursue leadership training, take risks, and try new approaches. It fails when it doesn't invest in the tools and technology needed to streamline processes, all because of budgetary concerns.

That's where *A Solution-Focused Culture* comes in. Through the story of Clearview, we've laid out a practical, real-world scenario to demonstrate how an organization can shift from a culture of rigid regulation to one focused on finding solutions. The book captures the building blocks necessary to create this cultural shift—one that empowers employees to think creatively and collaboratively and, ultimately, to enjoy their work more. By connecting people to solutions, both employees and customers benefit. Employees become more engaged, and the public receives the quality service they deserve.

As you move into the next sections, we'll provide a step-by-step guide for implementing the kind of transformation we witnessed in Clearview within your own organization. These six practical steps will give you the tools to turn your workplace into one that fosters leadership, innovation, and collaboration.

Thank you for joining us on this journey. We hope you found the story of Clearview insightful and that it provided you with a new perspective on how organizations can function better when they focus on solutions rather than obstacles. If you're looking for more resources, tools, or advice, please visit us at www.Solution-FocusedCulture.com.

Enjoy the rest of the book and best of luck in creating a solution-focused culture in your organization.

—*Tim Bolduc and Jessica Leavins*

CHAPTER 1
NEW BEGINNINGS, OLD BATTLES

The late-afternoon sun that often streamed through the window in TJ Strong's office was missing today, leaving his work space feeling somewhat melancholy. As he looked at the stack of spreadsheets that made up the half-completed budget lying on top of his desk, he listened to the rain beating on the window. A storm . . . what a fitting tribute to this day, he thought, but the storm outside was nothing compared to the hurricane of emotions that had passed through the office less than two hours ago. Sarah

Givens's termination had been more painful than he had anticipated.

As TJ placed his coffee cup in the microwave, the day's thoughts ran. Today, he'd fired someone who had been with the city longer than he had been in the workforce. He wouldn't normally drink coffee this late in the day, but today . . . today was no ordinary day. Sarah had once been a pillar of the organization but, over time, had become a roadblock where there should have been a pathway to progress. She was often unyielding and frustrating to anyone trying to do business in Clearview. Which had led to calls for change in the way the city did business. Tomorrow, employees and citizens alike would be shocked not to see her behind her desk. It hadn't been easy for him to send her home for good. Sure, he had been through tough employee conversations before, but all his experience had not quite prepared him for the weight of telling someone they no longer had a place in an organization they'd served for most of their adult life.

Now standing alone in his office, TJ found himself reflecting on the path that had led him here. Just a few months ago, he was managing his own small business and consulting for several construction firms. His experience had always been on the other side of the counter and outside the realm of government. He specialized in organizational efficiency, growth strategies, and performance improvement, and he was pretty good at it. His private sector background had taught him how to lead teams and solve complex problems, but transitioning into public service brought challenges he hadn't anticipated.

TJ could never have guessed how set in their ways tenured government employees could be. Before the last few weeks, he thought the construction industry was a challenge, but he quickly learned it had nothing on small-town politics. Yet, the opportunity to help shape the future of a city he'd loved since before marrying his beautiful wife and settling down was one he couldn't ignore.

At forty-five, TJ had already built a successful career, but Clearview—or at least the idea of what it could become—held a special place in his heart. He and his wife, Dawn, were raising their three kids in the same community he had grown up in. His son, Parker, was ten and active in city-league sports, playing on the same fields he had played on. Liberty, at only seven, loved to dance and was learning to sing and play the guitar. The youngest, Adeline, was a precocious five-year-old who loved soccer and visiting the library for Crafts with Kids Days.

Clearview was experiencing rapid growth, which had stretched its infrastructure and workforce to the breaking point in recent years. TJ had witnessed firsthand that the community was starting to feel the strain. The burden of this growth was evident when he saw the condition of the league fields his kids played on and the roads he took to get to the games. Resources were stretched, attitudes were poor, and taxpayers were tired of it. These are the types of indicators that scream an organization is in trouble, and at Clearview, they were screaming so loud the city council had to pay attention.

It was hard to believe that it had only been six months since city councilman Tommy Goodspeed approached TJ to ask if it was possible to change the culture of a government operation. The meeting was shortly after hearing TJ speak at the Gulf Coast Business Development Seminar. That night, TJ delivered his presentation entitled The Importance of a Good Organizational Culture. TJ had given this presentation several times, and it was always good to talk to attendees after, but this time was different. Halfway through their conversation, Tommy asked the question that would change TJ's life. "The city of Clearview has decided to hire a city manager to help manage the growth. Do you think you might be interested in applying?" If Tommy had not specifically asked him that question, it never would have crossed his mind.

After a two-hour conversation with Tommy that night and some prodding from his wife over the next week, it started to feel like a natural next step and a place where he could potentially help. Councilman Goodspeed had convinced TJ that his background would equip him to make a difference and that he believed TJ could breathe new life into the city of Clearview.

After several weeks of prayer and contemplation, he took the plunge into public service. The application process involved a series of public interviews where he was asked dozens of questions about how he would improve the efficiency of Clearview's operations. None of his answers included firing a tenured employee . . .

The events of earlier today proved that despite TJ's confidence, stepping into the role of city manager would most definitely be more difficult than he had expected. Many long-standing employees were either resistant to change or had already left, leaving critical departments understaffed and unmotivated. The exodus of qualified employees had a crippling effect on operations, while the remaining low performers only made it worse. This trend with the employees was one of the first challenges TJ was tasked with addressing. It had already become clear that fostering a positive culture was vital to stabilizing the organization. TJ knew he had the skills and experience to turn things around, but it would take a delicate balance of understanding the city's unique challenges and applying the principles he had honed in the private sector. He had been hired to deliver solutions—and the city desperately needed them.

He took a sip from the cup he had been holding. The bitterness of the lukewarm coffee intensified the tension in his chest. Twenty-eight years of service, TJ thought to himself, *man*, that is a long time.

Sarah had started as the receptionist in building inspections and eventually worked her way up to leading her own department. Over the years, she had become a master at hiring emerging talent and keeping her department's budget balanced. Her specific skill seemed to serve Clearview well during the hard times when the economy was slow. With budgets tight and little to no activity, her conservative nature showed its true value, while her less-than-helpful nature went largely unnoticed. Times were changing, the local economy had rebounded, and stagnation was not an option for Clearview.

The city was growing at an incredible rate, whether they wanted it to or not, and the present challenges had outpaced her ability to manage them. Big companies were opting out of Clearview, stating it was too difficult to do bus-iness with the city and instead going to neighboring communities. The businesses that did come were often the less desired ones and typically did not have the much-coveted high-paying jobs that could keep talented youth from leaving home after college. There seemed to be little or no opportunities for further economic growth. The best businesses were going elsewhere, and the citizens of Clearview were tired of it.

Ms. Givens was hesitant to embrace the city's transformation. The quaint, small-town environment she thrived in was gone, and she didn't like what was coming, *or* maybe the complexity of the work had passed her by . . . Either way, the city was in trouble, and her time had run out. The oversight of the city's planning and development activities now required not only more technical expertise but also a willingness to acclimate to the times. New development systems require the ability to adapt to changes. Online applications and electronic plan submittals were the more efficient tools for permitting a project, but under her leadership, Clearview did not conform to the changes in the market.

Unfortunately, Sarah had shown no desire to put in the

work to change. In her mind, she was good enough; the city was getting by just fine. Everyone else just needed to understand that's the way it would be, and that was perfectly OK. Her resistance to change was undeniable, and it became clear during their first few meetings that she had little interest in the direction TJ was taking the city. The new direction came with professional leadership, new policies and procedures, and, most importantly, a new attitude.

He had tried—*Lord, he had tried*—to get her on board. He believed in giving struggling employees opportunities for growth, especially those like Sarah, who had been brought up in an organization that did not prepare them to be successful. Sarah's was a cautionary tale; someone gets a job in local government, performs well at the functional part of the job, and is eventually promoted. This happens multiple times in their career until they have been promoted beyond their professional or leadership ability, with little or no training to fall back on. He had seen it before, and it seldom ended well. No matter how much he wanted to see her succeed, it didn't take long for Sarah to make her position clear.

"I can't follow someone who doesn't know anything about government," she had said at their last meeting, "and if you continue to try to take Clearview in this direction, I *will* put an end to it. I knew hiring a city manager was a bad idea. I can't believe they went so far as to pick one with no government experience! You think we should just tell everyone, "Yes." That's not our job . . . we are regulators. You don't know what you are doing."

TJ remembered asking, "Doesn't the term *public servant* imply we are here to serve *the* public?"

Sarah had quipped back, "Like I said, I can't and won't follow someone who knows nothing about government.

In the month following this conversation, Sarah continued to make it evident that she had no intention of changing. She would ignore requests and even huff or make noises during department meetings when she disagreed with TJ. When he received a call from a developer this morning about a conversation she had had with Sarah, TJ knew it was time.

Roxanne Hartly, the developer for Partial Foods, had said, "We really wanted to come to Clearview, but our development team just believes we can't afford to lose the time it will take to get through your development order process." TJ remembered the sinking feeling he felt when she continued, "Ms. Givens just seemed determined to tell us no." TJ apologized and took Roxanne's number, promising to call her back with some solutions.

"They ran out of time to submit revisions," Sarah had barked back when TJ asked for clarification on what had happened. "If you can't follow the rules, then we can't process your paperwork. Besides, Clearview is not the right place for them."

It was at that moment that TJ made the final decision. He had been considering it for some time, but when he heard "out of time" and "not the right place," he determined that those words described Sarah and not Partial Foods. TJ tried to make the conversation as painless as possible, but difficult conversations are just that: difficult.

Sarah's last words as she walked out of his office were, "You don't know what you are doing."

Those words echoed in his mind. TJ had heard the sentiment before, not just from Sarah but from others in the city who were wary of his private sector background. He understood their skepticism. After all, before joining the City of Clearview, he was a small business owner and a consultant, not a career bureaucrat. His expertise was in turning around small businesses, ensuring profitability, and advising construction companies, not navigating the nuances of municipal governance.

All of that aside, the city council had hired him for a reason: Clearview needed a fresh perspective. The city was experiencing a phase of rapid growth that was overwhelming its infrastructure and staff. They had watched some of the best opportunities for economic growth go to their neighbors while they struggled to land the most basic businesses. Sure, they were still seeing growth, but it was population growth without the stores or industry Clearview desperately needed. Housing developments were being built left and right, but the citizens felt like they were watching their chances for substantial economic growth pass them by. Worse yet, qualified employees had been leaving in droves, worn down by outdated processes, an unintentional culture, and poor leadership practices that made them dread coming to work every day.

The first month after his arrival, TJ conducted a survey of all current employees and those who had recently resigned in hopes of finding something he could fix in the culture. Very few answered, and the sentiment was the same: they just did not feel fulfilled in the work they did.

TJ's mandate was clear: fix the culture, modernize the systems, and make Clearview a city that could thrive in this new era of expansion.

He just hadn't expected his first big move to be firing someone well-known within the organization. She was a fixture to citizens, business owners, and the city council alike.

Walking over to the sink and pouring out the coffee that had begun to turn his stomach, he remembered the words his long-time colleague Mark Wells had told him over the phone when he had called looking for advice about the decision to let Sarah go. "You gotta remember they are doing this to themselves," Mark had said in his Southern drawl. "You're just delivering the message." Mark's words from that day rang in TJ's head as he stood there. The words fell flat the day he first heard them . . . and again today, they made him feel no better for the act he knew was necessary.

A knock at the door broke the silence, startling TJ. It was

Christine Dutton, his executive assistant. "You good, Boss?" she asked, her voice soft but filled with concern. Christine was a faithful ally. She had worked in government long enough to know what had happened and even understood why.

He managed a tight smile. "It's OK. It's just been a crazy day."

"I can imagine," she said, stepping into the office. "The word is out. Social media has nothing on the city hall grapevine."

Of course, he knew about the city hall grapevine. He and Christine had joked that the previous public information officer had said the gossip system inside city hall needed its own name, something like City Holla.

"Yeah. I can't say I am surprised. I promise it wasn't easy. What is on the vine?" TJ said with a bit of apprehension.

Christine took a breath, her genuine concern evident. "Most people are not surprised, but some are worried this is the beginning of some big plan you have to clean house."

"Great," TJ said sarcastically. "That's not the plan at all."

"I think they know that you did what you had to do. Sarah has been," Christine paused for a moment, then finished with, "*struggling* for a while now."

"That's true. But to be honest, that didn't make it any easier. I know the employees are already nervous, and I really didn't want to start this way. I don't want people to think I'm the proverbial ax man. I'm here to fix the culture and stop talent from leaving, and in my first few months, I am showing someone the door," TJ said with reservation in his voice.

"*I* don't think you're the ax man, so at least that is not everyone," she chided. "You should stop exaggerating," Christine added with a knowing smile. "People are going to talk. Change is hard, especially for a city that's been stuck in its ways for so long. *Trust me*," she continued, "you had to do something." Then, adding her customary sarcasm, she said,

A SOLUTION-FOCUSED CULTURE

"But I would recommend coming up with a plan quick, or it's going to be just me and you around here, and I have enough to do just keeping you straight."

TJ appreciated her words, but more than the words, he appreciated her understanding that he had a job to do. Forcing a bit of a smile, he said, "That's true. It would be a tough gig, just the two of us around here. I mean, who would keep me straight if you had real work to do? I will just have to tighten up. That said . . . *you* should stop exaggerating; they will get rid of me long before everyone leaves." His smile broadened.

As Christine turned to leave, TJ's mind wandered back to the moment Sarah had walked out of his office, her face a mix of surrender and bitterness. He had seen that look before. It was the face of someone who felt like the world had passed them by and they couldn't catch up. It also was the face of someone who was probably not going to go easily.

TJ was challenging her life's work with the changes he was making, and by terminating her, he was taking away her purpose. To her, this was personal. Sarah wasn't a bad person, he reminded himself. She was just . . . out of place.

Clearview needed more—it deserved more. It needed good jobs, additional infrastructure, more parks, and safe places to live. Oh, and getting decent service with a smile should not be too much to ask. If TJ was going to be successful in changing Clearview, he would have to start with the culture at city hall. To do that, difficult decisions like today's would be part of the job.

As the door clicked shut behind Christine, she called back, "I'm headed out. You get some rest tonight, Boss. Tomorrow is going to be a big day."

TJ sat down at his desk. It still did not feel quite right. Checking his watch to find it was just past 5:00 p.m., he knew he had a long night ahead of him. Tomorrow would be about meeting with staff and reassuring the employees that everything would be fine. At some point in the very near future, a decision would have to be made about who would head up Sarah's department while he looked for a replacement. Rick Christopher, the planning manager, seemed to be a good pick; he was smart, helpful, and very technically qualified. He also seemed to get that his department was inefficient. "Yeah," TJ thought, "Rick will be good, even if it's only as the interim."

It was time to call Dawn and let her know he would be late. She would understand—she always did. She appreciated that TJ tried very hard to spend most nights with her and the kids. It was easy for him. He thoroughly enjoyed reviewing homework, attending ball games, or driving the carpool to youth group—well, maybe not the homework part, but definitely the rest of being a dad. But tonight it would have to wait; there was just too much work to do.

Sarah was gone, but everything was just getting started. There were some apparent problems, as evidenced by the employee engagement surveys he had been reviewing over the last few days. How could he explain the problems and how to fix them to the team? There had to be more to this than just an unwillingness to accept a new direction. Heck, he thought to himself, do I even know what the new direction is?

TJ told himself, "I have to put my thoughts together." Clearview wasn't going to fix itself overnight. At least the most challenging part was behind him.

Or so he hoped . . .

CHAPTER 2
THE AFTERMATH

TJ's phone was buzzing on his desk before his first sip of coffee Friday morning. It was still quite early; the sun was barely rising over the Clearview skyline. The screen was flashing "Tommy Goodspeed." Mr. Goodspeed was the city councilman who had convinced TJ to leave the private sector and take on the role of city manager. TJ knew this call was coming.

"Morning, Councilman," TJ said, leaning back in his chair, trying to sound composed despite the tension.

Goodspeed wasted no time. "TJ, what in the world is going on? My phone has been ringing all night and into this morning with people calling about Sara Givens. You fired her?"

TJ let out a breath. He had expected the fallout, but hearing the concern in Tommy's voice still stung. "I did. Look, I know it's not the way we wanted to start, but Sarah was standing in the way of every change we need to make. She wasn't on board with the new direction, and I couldn't ignore that."

Goodspeed paused. "I understand that. But, TJ, you were brought in to fix the culture, not oust long-standing employees. People are already nervous; we're hemorrhaging talent, and starting with a termination—especially someone who's been here as long as Sarah—doesn't exactly send a calming message."

"I hear you, Tommy," TJ replied, standing up and pacing the floor in his office. "But Sarah wasn't just resistant—she was actively undermining progress. Her attitude was feeding the problem. We need leaders who are committed to moving forward, not holding us back. I've got to think long-term here, and sometimes that means making tough calls."

"You need to make darn sure you're not creating more chaos," Goodspeed warned. "People are already uneasy with all the changes happening in Clearview. We don't want them thinking the new city manager is here to clean house."

"I'm not," TJ said firmly. "But I am here to create a team that's ready for where we're headed. I'll smooth things over with the staff today."

Less than an hour later, TJ stood at the head of the conference table, facing the department heads. The atmosphere was thick with apprehension. Everyone knew about Sarah's sudden departure, and now they were waiting to hear what was next or, worse yet, *who* was next.

TJ paused for a moment, surveying the room before he addressed the inevitable topic on everyone's mind: Sarah's termination. He knew the gravity of the decision, and while he was confident it had been the right move, the shockwave it sent through city hall was undeniable. Before diving into the discussion, TJ took a deep breath and let his eyes move around the table, reflecting on the unique strengths and challenges of each department head.

Jamie Lunds, the Human Resources director, was seated closest to him. In her mid-thirties and fresh into her role, Jamie already demonstrated immense potential. She had a master's degree in human resources and plenty of relevant experience, but what really stood out to TJ was her passion for the employees. Although she had only been with the city for a few months, Jamie had grown up in Clearview and carried with her a deep-rooted understanding of the community's needs and dynamics. She was sharp and organized and fully bought into making Clearview a better place to work. With her eagerness to be part of the solution, TJ knew Jamie would be one of his most reliable allies. Her excitement when it came to helping people and improving the culture was unmistakable.

Next to Jamie sat Darnell Williams, the Parks and Recreation director and, in many ways, the heart of the executive leadership cadre. As John Maxwell would say, Darnell was the "influential leader" of the group, like the captain of a baseball team, and the other department heads would likely follow him once he was on board. At thirty-five, Darnell was young and brimming with enthusiasm, the kind of guy who made people feel at ease just by walking into the room. He was great at inspiring people, and his employees loved him. As a local kid, he was instrumental in helping Clearview High School win state and then was off to college in the Midwest. At Midwest University, he played as the starting third baseman. After college, he was drafted and played a brief stint in the minor leagues. But his roots in Clearview ran deep, and following a career-ending injury, he returned home to take up the role of Parks and Recreation director. With his wife and newborn daughter, Darnell was fully committed to the town and saw his work as more than just a job—it was a way to give back to the community that had shaped him. Though he lacked extensive management experience, Darnell's eagerness to learn and drive to create meaningful opportunities for the town's youth made him a vital piece of the city's future. TJ appreciated Darnell's likability and knew he would play a significant role in developing recreational programs that could serve as a model for other small cities. But more than that, if he bought in, the rest would too.

A SOLUTION-FOCUSED CULTURE

Across from Darnell was Carrie Smith, the Finance director, a steady hand in the room and a professional who had been with the city for about fifteen years. A loving grandmother of two, Carrie was a seasoned financial expert with a short career in the private sector before trans-itioning to municipal work. Prior to coming to Clearview, Carrie had worked for a neighboring County Clerk of Court's office as a lead accountant. Her methodical approach to budgeting and finance was a blessing, and TJ was relieved to have her on board. He knew that she would keep them on track financially and help him stay out of hot water. That said, Carrie was risk-averse, preferring to stick with what had worked in the past rather than embracing innovation. She rarely advocated for spending on things she deemed unnecessary—like off-site meetings, new technology, or even employee training programs. For Carrie, the goal was to keep the city's finances in order, minimize risk, and avoid anything that could jeopardize the bottom line. TJ respected her diligence, but he was also aware that her reluctance to invest in staff development and large-scale capital improvement projects might clash with the changes he needed to make. To get the staff at Clearview up to speed, they would need to invest in training, both technical and professional. Additionally, if they were going to court large retailers and the desired high-paying employment-providing industries, Clearview would have to invest in building the roads and utilities necessary to support growth. Carrie's service had been exemplary, and she would want to finish out her career with as few disruptions as possible. TJ needed her and was committed to working hard to convince her that spending in certain areas was an asset, not a liability.

Then there was Kevin Ashton, the fire chief, a man nearing the twilight of his career. At sixty-three, Kevin had been with the Clearview Fire Department for thirty-three years, having started at the age of thirty following a twelve-year career in the air force serving as a fireman. He had worked his way through the ranks at Clearview, earning the respect of the department and the community alike. However, as skilled as Kevin was at firefighting, his enthusiasm for the administrative side of the job had dwindled over time. He preferred being in the field and maintaining camaraderie with his team.

To TJ, Kevin did not seem thrilled about the prospect of changes or new programs, especially with his planned retirement just five years away. Kevin's wife, Milly, was set to retire from the school board around the same time, and their sights were firmly set on a future filled with relaxation. The last thing he was thinking about was navigating the intricacies of organizational change. TJ understood that motivating Kevin to embrace a new city-wide direction would be a challenge, but he also knew Kevin loved the firefighters he worked with, and this community and his experience were invaluable. It would be worth the work.

Frank Cannon, the police chief, sat quietly at the other end of the table, always serious, always focused. He had joined the Clearview Police Department twelve years ago, coming from a small community where he had served as a lieutenant. When Frank first arrived, the department had been understaffed and overwhelmed by a myriad of issues that had eroded public trust. But Frank had slowly turned things around. He built a stronger force, addressing the department's most critical problems head-on. Frank was a man of few words, but his results spoke for themselves. With eight years left before his own retirement, Frank's priority was ensuring the department had the resources and facilities it needed to succeed long after he left. The top of his current priorities included repairs or replacement of the public safety building. While Frank had never come out and said anything, TJ thought that he had seen a reservation in him about the way TJ approached addressing shortfalls in the operations of Clearview. Frank had been leading his team his way, and they were getting it done. He wasn't necessarily opposed to TJ's vision for the city, but neither was he interested in undoing any of the work he had put in at the police department. It seemed that his focus remained squarely on his department's operational needs, and he liked it that way.

Finally, there was Walter Wooden, the Public Works director and perhaps the department head currently serving the city the longest. With thirty-five years under his belt, Walter was the embodiment of old-school dedication. He knew his job and his department better than anyone, but his lack of formal leadership training and his absence of a college degree left him feeling a bit insecure, especially with a new city manager who clearly had big ideas. The reservations Walter felt before the termination would likely be much stronger now. Walter wanted the city to succeed, and, deep down, he knew that change was needed. But he also cared deeply about his legacy and protecting the work he had done over the past three decades. TJ was sure that Sarah leaving was more than a little unnerving for Walter, since they had worked side by side as friends and come up in the organization together. Balancing his desire for continuity with TJ's push for change would require tact and trust, and TJ was ready to build both.

As he prepared to address them all, TJ took a deep breath. Inside, he was asking himself what he had gotten himself into.

"Alright, team, let's address the elephant in the room," TJ began. "Yesterday, I made the decision to part ways with Sarah. I didn't make it lightly, and I know it's unsettling when someone who's been with the city for so long is no longer part of the team. But the truth is, we can't move forward with people who aren't fully committed to where we need to go."

A few of the department heads exchanged uneasy glances, but no one spoke. TJ continued, his voice steady, "I'm not here to slash jobs or to shake things up just for the sake of it. But I *am* here to change the culture and to focus on solutions, collaboration, and serving the people of Clearview better. I need all of you on board for that. If we're going to slow the loss of talent and get this city back on track, we've got to start working together."

Chief Ashton looked around the room at his colleagues and said, "Help me understand what you mean when you say change the culture." Several of the others nodded their heads. He continued, "I mean, we are all for improving, but Sarah has been here for a long time. I think we all are wondering who is next."

TJ appreciated the concerns of the team, so he reiterated his earlier point: "No, like I said, I am not here to slash jobs. When I say change the culture, I mean that we need to get back to serving the public. I want us to start focusing on answers, asking ourselves how we can help people and what we can do to connect our citizens to solutions."

The tension in the room eased slightly, but TJ could tell there was still concern. He softened his tone. "I know change is hard, and I'm not going to pretend it'll happen overnight. But we have an opportunity here to build something great. And I'm here to support you in that—every step of the way."

The rest of the day was spent walking through the halls, visiting various departments and talking one-on-one with staff. TJ's first stop after the department head meeting was to visit Rick Christopher, the city planner. Rick was thirty-five years old with two kids, a graduate of the University of Florida with a degree in planning. Rick was intelligent, efficient, and well-liked by the planning team and the public alike. He had worked with Sarah for several years and at the beginning of the conversation with TJ was very concerned about his future with the city. TJ could feel the unease as he talked with Rick about filling in for Sarah while he looked for a replacement.

"I am hopeful you can fill in as the department head for the planning department," TJ said.

A SOLUTION-FOCUSED CULTURE

"Yes, sir, I will do whatever you need," Rick said. "I would like to discuss how you want me to handle issues that come up. Sarah liked to have input on all major decisions. Do you want me to bring them to you now?"

TJ encouraged Rick, "I am confident you can handle whatever comes up. Of course, if you want my input, just come by, and we will discuss it. But if you are confident with your decision, believe it is what is best for the customer, and is in line with the rules, then you are free to make the decision." TJ handed Rick a piece of paper with his cell phone number on it, saying, "Rick, just call me if you need anything."

"Will do!" Rick said.

TJ started to walk away, but turning back, he said, "I would like for you to start attending our department head meetings and working with the rest of the leadership team. Christine will get you all the details."

"That sounds good, and I am looking forward to it," Rick said.

As he made his way through the halls, TJ took time to chat with anyone who looked like they had something to say. He wanted to make sure everyone had a chance to voice their concerns and, more importantly, to understand why the changes were necessary. He was surprised at how many people were open about their concerns.

At each stop, TJ took his time, sitting down with the staff and explaining his vision. He talked about how Sarah's departure wasn't about eliminating people or the beginning of a big plan to remove employees. He emphasized that he wasn't looking for people to fear for their jobs, but to embrace the future they were building together. Each time he sat down with a team member, he gained confidence that everything would be OK.

Every opportunity to chat for any length of time, TJ would ask the employee, "What do you see the mission of the city to be?" More often than not, he found that the employees lacked a unified vision and an understanding of what the mission was. Sure, they could talk about their jobs and what they did every day, but the "why" behind it was missing. TJ ended all the impromptu meetings the same way: he promised to come back and spend more time in each department to learn more about what they do.

As the day went on, TJ could sense a shift in the air. People were still cautious, but the more time he spent with them, the more they seemed interested in what he had to say. As employees got more comfortable in the conversation, they would ask questions about the direction the city was headed or what changes he envisioned. TJ would just assure them that he was still evaluating what changes were needed but that no matter what the final decisions were, the employees would be a part of it. By the time the sun dipped below the horizon, TJ had spoken to most of the staff, reassuring them that while things were changing, the goal was to make Clearview a better place for them to work and, by doing so, a better place to live, work, and play for its citizens.

Making his way back to his office, he knew that the road ahead wouldn't be easy. Change was never comfortable, but with the right approach, he could help the city move beyond its past and build the culture it desperately needed.

As he passed Christine's desk, she said with a worried look, "You left your phone on your desk. Ms. Bolder called. She said you could call her tomorrow . . . but I got the sense today would be better."

"OK, I'll call her now," TJ said, picking up his phone to find several missed calls and text messages. While scrolling through the notifications, he said, "Hey, Christine, what is Clearview's mission?"

Poking her head around the door frame, she said, "Do you mean what is the mission statement?"

"I'll take that, but really, I am curious about our why. I mean, what is the mission here?" TJ said thoughtfully.

"I am not sure we have a mission statement, but I would say our mission should be to help our citizens have a better life," Christine said with some confidence, then asked, "How's that?"

"That's a good mission, but I think it's time we get a city-wide understanding of what our mission is," TJ said confidently, "Please work on setting up a special workshop with all the city council and the department heads for some time next week. We need a mission!"

"Will do. I am thinking a week from Tuesday will be the earliest we can make that happen," Christine said with some hesitation.

"Perfect!" TJ said. "I better get on this call with Ms. Bolder."

"Sounds good. Oh, I set up several 'ride-alongs' for you next week, one with each department. If you don't need anything, I am headed out," Christine said as she took her keys from her purse and shut down her computer.

"Perfect, thanks! I will see you next week," TJ said as he dialed Ms. Bolder's number, bracing for more pushback.

CHAPTER 3
IN THE TRENCHES

It was early Monday morning when TJ Strong strolled into city hall, doughnuts in hand, ready to immerse himself in the daily grind of Clearview's operations. His plan for the week was simple: learn the ins and outs of each department by working alongside the staff. TJ knew if he was going to develop a plan to turn things around, he would have to get to know the people behind the desks, the "boots on the ground," and understand the processes that kept the city running.

They were right when they said he did not know government from the inside, and while he did believe that all organizations are pretty much the same, he needed to see firsthand the challenges his employees faced. He also really needed to understand where the gaps in customer service were most glaring.

Christine had set up his first ride-along with the Facilities Department, where maintenance staff managed the upkeep of city buildings and infrastructure. From the moment he walked in, TJ could feel a sense of frustration in the air. The crew seemed capable, but their energy was stifled. In the main room, there was a board with projects listed on it. TJ noticed that nearly all the projects were in the "in progress" phase, with a note that said, "Waiting on approval." From the board, it appeared that no matter what the problem was, whether it was a light fixture needing repair or an air conditioning unit that had malfunctioned, the maintenance staff would immediately stop and consult their supervisor before making even minor decisions.

"Hey, guys, help me understand this project board," TJ said as he set the box of doughnuts on the table.

Jim Adams, the maintenance foreman, sighed heavily as he explained to TJ, "We could fix half these issues on our own, but protocol says everything needs approval. By the time we get the green light, the problem's either worse or already fixed. To be honest, sometimes people in the department just fix it themselves instead of waiting on us. I don't blame them for being annoyed. It's frustrating for me. Sure, I want to help them, but I also have to follow the rules."

Jim's building resentment for the system resonated with TJ. These employees had the skills to solve problems quickly, but the bureaucracy slowed them down, making them feel powerless. Staff members who should have been empowered to take the initiative were discouraged by a rigid chain of command. Unnecessary layers of supervision choked the department's efficiency, and morale had clearly taken a hit. TJ spent several hours going from project to project with the team. As he was getting ready to go on his next ride-along, he made a mental note: "This department needs more autonomy, not only to get the work done but also to have *any* job satisfaction."

"Jim, what do you think about taking a look at the policies and getting back with Walter and me to discuss potential changes?" TJ asked Jim before leaving.

"Sure, I wouldn't mind that at all. But I don't want to create any waves," Jim answered with some reservations.

"Don't worry about that. Just make a list of a couple of

policies that make the process less efficient, and we will discuss them," TJ said. "And thanks, man, for everything you do. We appreciate you."

"Alright, Mr. Strong. I will see you later," Jim replied.

After lunch, Christine had TJ working with the Utility Billing Department. Immediately, it began to feel like more of the same issues. The software the staff used to process payments was outdated and cumbersome, requiring excessive manual input and paperwork for every transaction.

"This system is a nightmare," one employee named Carol Raspberry confided to TJ. "Half the time, we're just re-entering the same data multiple times. And all this paperwork we print? It just gets tossed later—no one ever looks at it."

"If no one looks at it, why do we do it?" TJ inquired.

"Your guess is as good as mine," Carol mused. "All I know is we were doing it when I got here and will probably be doing it when I retire in ten years." Looking around before continuing, she said, "Don't get me started on how the customers feel about it. I would be irritated, too, if I had to put the same information on four different forms just to get my water turned on. I mean, once you tell us who you are, where you want service, and where to send the bill, it gets pretty simple from there. But do you think we stop there . . . *nope*! We have reams of paper with information no one needs. If you ask me, I could streamline this process down to one page and a happy customer, but what do I know?" Carol laughed out loud.

TJ was familiar with this refrain from his work in the private sector: unnecessary processes that did little to add value but were somehow ingrained in the system. These processes were frequently put in place by people who had either never done the actual job or were so many years disconnected from practice that they forgot what it was like to actually *do* the work. The toll it took on the staff was obvious.

They were drowning in paperwork that seemed to serve no purpose, and their frustrations were clear.

"Is there anything else we should look at?" TJ inquired.

"Did I mention this horrible software?" Carol snorted as she continued, "We can't even take payments online. Can you believe that? Everyone hates it!"

"Yeah, you mentioned the software, Carol, but I'll put a star by my note," TJ said with a smile.

"Good plan, Mr. Manager," Carol said, clearly distracted. "Well, the day is almost over, and I have to pick up my grandkid from daycare as soon as I get off. It was nice to meet you."

As Carol started packing up her things for the day, TJ asked, "Carol, thanks for letting me hang out with you today. If we put together a process improvement team to look at some of these concerns, would you be willing to help out?"

With some surprise and what looked like some half-hearted interest, she said, "Sure, I would love to, as long as it's not like last time."

"What happened last time?" TJ inquired.

"Nothing, *Boss*, that's what happened . . . *nothing*." Carol shook her head as she left for the day.

The inefficiencies TJ identified on the first day riding along with staff not only hindered the employees but also frustrated customers who had to wait longer for simple tasks to be completed. He knew that streamlining the billing system and cutting down on redundant paperwork would be a key step in improving the department's workflow. He also knew that before he started something, he better be ready to finish it.

The next morning, TJ was shadowing the Building Inspections Department. Having consulted for several construction companies in the area, he felt like he was very familiar with the department. This one would be a challenge.

"I was able to get all of the councilmembers and department heads together for a workshop a week from today," Christine said. "I hope that is OK," she said. "I asked Jamie to help set this up."

"Sure, that's perfect. I plan to get her to help with the meeting," TJ said. "I will stop by to see her a little later to work out the details."

"That sounds good. Let me know what else you need," Christine said as she pointed to TJ's backpack, reminding him not to forget it. "You need to go now if you want to be on time."

"Got it. I am off to the building department," TJ said with a tone that said he was not sure how it would go.

Christine chastised him as he headed down the hall to meet the building official, "Play nice, Boss, and keep an open mind."

"You know me, I always play nice," TJ said, smirking, as he turned back around and stole a peanut butter cup from the candy jar sitting on the corner of her desk.

The morning started with a meeting to discuss what would be needed for a new national chain store to move into the vacant tenant space in a local shopping center. The shopping center, Evans Corner, had fallen into disrepair due to its owners' lack of maintenance and had been unable to land any decent anchor stores in recent years. For a shopping center to be successful, it needed a large, nationally known tenant to "anchor" it. Evan's Corner didn't have one and was having trouble even getting anyone to even think about coming. This would be a big deal for the community.

TJ had heard that the clothing store Thread Max was interested in investing in Clearview. Landing this retailer would be a huge win for the town. It was the practice for Thread Max to rent space in a dying shopping center. Every time they entered a market like the one at Evan's Corner, the company would invest in the building and surrounding site. The investment made typically completely revived the surrounding area. In addition to bringing revitalization and more shopping opportunities, it would also provide both full- and part-time jobs.

The meeting attendees included representatives from the building, fire, and planning departments, as well as the engineering firm from the shopping center. Once the meeting had begun, TJ watched in horror as it went from bad to worse. It was like his team came in ready to say no and moved farther and farther away from yes as the day went on. One city employee opened by stating, "I can't imagine anyone going into that building; it needs a ton of work." TJ was mortified.

As the day went on, he realized that the dynamic between the building and fire inspect-ors was adversarial at best. "It's like we're working against each other," Donald Owens, the building official, grumbled during a break. "A contractor comes to me for an answer to a question, and then the fire inspector will come and say something completely different. The poor guy leaves confused as heck."

TJ had observed firsthand how conflicting standards and communication breakdowns between departments created unnecessary headaches for potential projects. Instead of working together to guide customers through the process, the employees seemed more interested in defending their own territory. It was an "us versus them" mentality that had no place in an efficient organization. What should have been a collaborative effort between departments had turned into a bureaucratic tug-of-war, leaving customers stuck in the middle.

By the time TJ left the building department, he was questioning whether or not he could get this team to work together. He would be spending his afternoon with Rick in the planning department, and maybe he could find some answers there. First, he was going to get some lunch, and then he would try to figure out how to save the Thread Max deal.

"Welcome back, TJ," Rick said, greeting TJ as he returned from lunch. "What did you think of this morning's meeting?"

"Well, Rick, I have to be honest, I was pretty uncomfortable. I feel like the Thread Max deal is doable, but from the meeting, I don't think they will feel that way," TJ said, clearly concerned.

"I understand," Rick said. "Let's not bury it yet. I have some ideas. I can call the engineer; he is a good local guy. I'll help him with some of the challenges that came up today. We should be OK."

TJ was relieved. "Man, that is great news. Is it like that all the time?"

"Unfortunately, it is. The whole team is full of really good, smart, and capable professionals. It's just that we don't have a common goal." Rick said thoughtfully, "I like that you are coming around and seeing what we all do. I am hopeful it will help you see our challenges."

"I am too," TJ said. "I have already learned a lot. Now show me around the Planning Department."

Rick and TJ spent the next several hours touring the Planning Department, learning about each division's work. TJ was impressed by how much Rick understood about all the different divisions in the department and how well he knew the people. At each stop, Rick would share a little bit about the employee, how many kids they had, or what their spouse did for a living. He set his employees at ease with small talk. Then he would have them share with TJ what they did, as well as anything they found challenging about their jobs.

"This is Mr. Strong," Rick would say. "He is here to help us make our jobs better so we can serve the public better."

TJ had a brief but illuminating conversation with one of the staff members. Susan Lufkin, a senior planner, beamed when she talked about the joy she found in her work. "My favorite part of the job," she said, "is helping people bring their projects to life. When someone comes in with an idea

A SOLUTION-FOCUSED CULTURE

and we can help them navigate the process, it's really rewarding."

This was the kind of attitude TJ wanted to spread across all departments: a focus on service, problem-solving, and helping people succeed. But he knew that to get there, the city needed more than just good intentions. It needed a complete overhaul of its culture, starting with clearly defined core values and empowering employees like Susan to do what they did best.

Rick's approach to bringing TJ around set everyone at ease, and the afternoon proved to be enjoyable. By the time he headed back to his office, TJ started to consider making Rick the permanent planning director. He was not sure yet, but Rick really seemed to understand what TJ was looking for in a leadership role.

Wednesday morning started early as TJ joined the police officers for the 6:00 a.m. shift change. He arrived a few minutes early and headed to the breakroom for some wake-up juice. Chief Cannon was in there drinking coffee and eating a doughnut.

"I know," Cannon said with a smirk and continued, "it's a little stereotypical: cops and doughnuts. Here's a pro tip, TJ, avoid the powdered ones, or everyone will know you hit the power rings." He chuckled.

TJ said, "Thanks for the tip. I will keep that in mind."

Chief Cannon said, "Today, you will be riding with officer Brandon Simmons. He is a good cop. I really think he will give you some excellent insight into how the organization is operating."

"I appreciate you setting this up. I am looking forward to today," TJ replied.

Just after 6:00 a.m., the officers were filing out of the training room. Officer Simmons, a tall young man with a neat uniform and a close-cropped haircut, noticed TJ standing by the breakroom entrance. "Mr. Strong, I understand you'll be riding with me today," he said respectfully. "My patrol car is out back. Follow me."

As they patrolled the streets, Officer Simmons opened up about the challenges the department faced. "This place was a mess before Chief Cannon got here," Simmons said, recalling a time before his own tenure when the police department was embroiled in scandals. Though these issues had been resolved, the officers felt the reputation of the department was still tainted by the past. "Even though it happened long before I joined, it still feels like we're fighting that reputation every day."

TJ listened as Brandon explained the lingering sense of mistrust from the community and even within the department itself. The officer's frustration was profound.

He was part of a new generation of police, but the shadow of past mistakes hung over him and his colleagues. They needed a fresh start, a way to rebuild trust and redefine their purpose. As TJ sat in the patrol car, he realized just how deep-rooted the need for a city-wide shift in culture was. It wasn't just about processes; it was about healing divisions and setting clear, unifying goals. It was about giving the team something they could believe in.

A SOLUTION-FOCUSED CULTURE

By the time Wednesday afternoon rolled around, TJ had gathered a clearer picture of the internal struggles. He had seen departments working in silos, employees feeling bogged down by rigid rules, and a general sense of disconnection from the city's mission. He was deep in thought, reviewing his notes from his ride-along with Officer Simmons, when his phone buzzed. A name flashed on the phone screen: councilmember Stephanie Harris. TJ took a deep breath before answering, knowing that any call from Ms. Harris was likely to involve pressure for quick results.

"TJ, I just got off the phone with a friend of mine, a builder," Ms. Harris started without pleasantries. "He's having a miserable time getting his inspections done and says there's been nothing but delays and confusion between the building and fire inspectors. What's going on over there?"

TJ had anticipated this call since spending Tuesday in the Building Inspections Department. The tension between the building inspectors and fire inspectors was clear. They were stepping on each other's toes and creating a mess for anyone caught in the middle, especially builders trying to meet deadlines. It was exactly the kind of situation that Harris had campaigned against, and TJ knew she'd be quick to push for change.

"I've seen it firsthand," TJ replied, leaning back in his chair. "The inspectors are all really good people with a lot of expertise. That said, the communication breakdown between the inspectors is something I've been looking into. They're more focused on protecting their own turf than working together, and it's causing headaches for customers like your friend."

"That's not good enough, TJ," Harris snapped. "These builders aren't just getting headaches; they're losing money. And that reflects poorly on all of us. I ran on a platform of efficiency, and I expect results. What are you doing about it?"

TJ sighed internally but kept his voice calm. "I understand

your frustration, Ms. Harris, and I'm already working on addressing these issues. This week, I've been going from department to department, getting a real feel for the obstacles in our processes. It's not just about inspections—there's a culture here of regulation, when it should be one of service. It is in every department, and it's something I plan to change."

There was a pause on the other end of the line before Harris spoke again, her tone slightly softer. "I get that there's a lot to fix, but TJ, people are watching . . . I am watching . . . And we don't have time to waste. These kinds of delays and excuses are exactly what I campaigned against."

"I hear you," TJ replied. "And I'm not ignoring it. But real change takes time. I'm building relationships with the department heads, and we're going to start from the ground up—redefine our values, streamline processes, and get everyone on the same page. I promise you, we'll see improvement, but we need to make sure the changes we implement are sustainable."

"Alright," Ms. Harris finally conceded, although she didn't sound entirely convinced. "But make it quick. I've got more builders calling me every day, and they won't wait forever."

"I understand," TJ said. "I'll keep you updated as we move forward."

After the call ended, TJ couldn't shake the pressure building on his shoulders. Ms. Harris wasn't wrong. The city was in dire need of efficiency, and the longer the status quo remained, the more frustrated Clearview's builders, developers, and residents would become. He thought back to his ride-along with Officer Simmons and how the department still carried the burden of past scandals. It was clear that the city needed a cultural reset, not just an improvement in processes, but to redefine what it meant to serve the community.

Thursday morning, TJ was headed to Public Works to meet with Mary Daniels, the city engineer. She was eager to show him some of the bottlenecks developers faced. They walked through a recently permitted project together. Mary was intelligent and full of creative ideas, but TJ could sense that she, like many others in the city, was frustrated by the system she operated within. When they got back to Public Works after completing inspections, Mary mentioned in passing how much easier it would be if she had more autonomy in resolving issues on-site rather than running everything through layers of bureaucracy.

"It's like we're stuck in neutral," she said, sounding slightly exasperated. "I know how to solve the problems our customers face, but we're so tied down by protocol that we can't be as effective as we should be."

TJ nodded, thinking back to the conversation with Ms. Harris. It wasn't just Mary; it was the entire organization. Everyone was waiting for permission to act, hesitant to make decisions without approval. This mindset was leading to the very inefficiencies Harris had brought up on the phone.

TJ's week concluded with a visit to the Parks and Recreation Department, where he saw a different kind of customer service. One of the staff members, Teri Lamont, had stepped up to help a mom struggling to fill out paperwork for her child's soccer registration. "I hope it's OK I did that," Teri said when TJ asked about it. "She just looked like she needed a hand."

"It's more than OK," TJ said, smiling. "That's exactly what we should be doing: helping people."

Teri's actions were a breath of fresh air and, for TJ, a reminder of what the city could be. He realized that what Teri had done was so much more than just fill out a form. He had connected with the customer, offered a solution, and created a positive experience. It was the kind of customer service TJ wanted to see citywide: employees not just following rules, but actively working to solve problems.

As the week came to a close, TJ sat down with each of the

department heads. Over coffee and conversation, he shared his observations. Every department had its unique strengths, but the common theme was clear: there was no unified set of core values and no shared mission across the city. Each department was operating like its own kingdom, with their own priorities, procedures, and frustrations. Staff members didn't feel empowered to solve problems or collaborate across divisions. But despite these challenges, TJ saw potential. His conversations with employees like Mary showed him that the city was full of people who genuinely cared about serving the public.

TJ was exhausted but optimistic. There was no doubt that Clearview's departments were fragmented, and the culture needed a reset, but there were bright spots. Employees like Teri, Susan, and Mary showed him that the potential was there. They just needed to be given the right tools and the freedom to use them.

Sitting in his office late Friday night, TJ reflected on the week. There was still so much work to do, but the direction was clear. The pressure from Ms. Harris would continue, but TJ was confident that with the right approach, they could deliver the results she—and the people of Clearview—expected.

CHAPTER 4
STARTING WITH YES

Friday evening, TJ leaned back in his chair. A week had passed since Sarah Givens's infamous termination, and TJ was not feeling any better about his progress. After the last five days of meetings with staff, he was confident he had a good feel for the challenges the team faced and overall morale. The feeling wasn't good. As he sat in his awful desk chair that he hated, his phone began to buzz on the desk. Peeking at his watch and seeing 6:30 p.m., he knew immediately who it was.

"Hey, baby, what's up?" he said, knowing exactly what was up.

"Don't you 'hey baby' me, dude. You know exactly what's up," his wife said with a fake attitude. "We have plans, and they include my handsome husband. What are the chances you can send him home?"

TJ winced. He'd forgotten about the plans but did not dare to admit that to Dawn. Between the chaos at city hall and the monumental task ahead, he got lost in the work. How could he leave now? He didn't even have any idea how to phrase the problem. TJ knew he couldn't begin to solve something he could not even explain.

He needed to take all the information rolling around in his head from this week and put it together into something he could evaluate and develop a solution for.

"Baby, I am really swamped here. Is it too late to reschedule? Just blame me . . . your handsome husband . . ." he said in a playful tone. "They will understand."

There was a pause on the other end, and TJ braced himself.

"You've been working late every night this week," she said, her voice patient but firm. "I get it: this new job is huge, but *we* need to see you too. Not to mention, I do not want to eat with your sister and her husband without you there. I love them, but it's your family. Not to mention, the kids are excited about seeing their cousins tonight. Can I just tell them you will be late? You can meet us there."

TJ smiled. Dawn was such an amazing partner in life. She was always understanding, but when she was right, she was right, and tonight . . . she was right. "I can make that work. I'm onto something, so I want to get the thought on the board before I leave. The city's culture, it's broken—and if I don't fix it now, it'll just keep getting worse," TJ said, knowing it was true but also knowing that if he didn't figure it out soon, he might not be there to figure it out at all. The council was not very happy with the drop in morale. Sarah had more influence than TJ had expected, and while they were giving him some time, their patience was quickly shrinking.

His wife's tone softened. "You are going to get this. You just have to figure out how to get them off always saying no. Just don't forget about us in the process."

"I won't," he promised, though the weight of what he had to do still hung heavy. "I'll meet you all in an hour. I just need to get this down."

"OK," she said, resigned. "But don't forget dinner is at your favorite restaurant, Sam's Steakhouse. Unlike what you are dealing with there, the people at Sam's always make sure we have a great experience. No matter what we ask for, they figure out how to get us what we want. I guess they start off expecting to have solutions to get to yes," she said with a little ironic tone. "Bye. I love you, babe. See you soon."

"I love you, too, baby. See ya soon."

Her words lingered after they hung up: "They start off expecting solutions." It echoed in his mind as he returned to the whiteboard with a marker in hand. For years, Clearview had been operating under a default *no*. No to new ideas. No to solutions. No to taking risks. It was a knee-jerk reaction, the only reaction—no care for what people needed, what people wanted, or even what was best for the city. No was the place where everything started, and most ideas died. Heck, it had become part of the city's DNA.

He remembered his conversation with Sarah. "We are regulators," she had said. This was true: they did have a responsibility to make sure people followed the rules, but it had become an identity instead of a part of their responsibility. This adopted identity would have to change if they were ever going to build something sustainable.

The more he thought about it, the more he realized that the regulator identity had developed a "no" culture, which had become more than an attitude; it was a state of mind. Staff was conditioned to believe that their primary function was to make sure the applicant was complying with a policy. They had forgotten that being a public servant meant serving the public. TJ needed to get the staff to understand that the customer may not know exactly what they are looking for. He wanted the team to ask questions, dig into the customers' needs, and help them find an answer that both met policy and met the needs of the customer.

Maybe there was something to the way Sam's Steakhouse did business, something that set them apart from everyone else in the restaurant industry. He knew there was, and he needed to figure out what set them apart and whether he could duplicate it at Clearview.

TJ said out loud to no one, "What is it about Sam's that makes me love it so much?"

Replying to himself, he said, "When I ask them for something they don't have or can't do, they don't say no. Instead, they immediately start looking for solutions. They always ask, 'What exactly are you trying to get? Is there a flavor you are looking for? Maybe we can get you what you want, just a different way.'" TJ smiled, "That's it!"

Without thinking much further, TJ wrote at the top in big, bold letters:

THE PROBLEM: WE LOOK FOR WAYS TO SAY NO.

TJ circled it twice and then added underneath:

Learn to get to what the customer really needs. We will help them find a solution that works for them and us!

He stood there for a moment, staring at the words. Comfortable that he now knew what the starting point had to be, he began to feel a little better. Dawn had done it again: "I guess they start off expecting to have solutions and get to yes." For twenty-five years, she had been his inspiration. Tonight, she had done it again. This was a great beginning. It was a place to begin the reshaping process. He would change the way the city did business. Tomorrow, he would work out the details, but tonight, he would meet his amazing family for dinner.

An hour and a half later, TJ pulled up at Sam's Steakhouse for dinner with family and friends. As he walked in, Mikey, the business owner, noticed TJ coming in and walked over. "Ms. Strong and your family are over here in the back. It's good to see you, Mr. Strong."

"It's great to see you, Mikey," TJ said. "I am looking forward to a good dinner and some time with family."

"Mr. Strong, you will be happy to know we were able to find your favorite cut of steak. Let me know if you would like it tonight."

TJ turned to Mikey and said, "Man, I really appreciate you. I have to ask, with all the great stuff on the menu, why did you bother trying to find my favorite cut?"

"Sir, that's what we do. We love to find people what they are looking for. Nothing makes us happier," Mikey said with a smile. "Look around, I have the best job in the world. People come here needing something. They could have stayed home and cooked their own meals or picked another restaurant in town, but, no, they trusted us to get them what they needed. We take that trust very seriously and find great joy exceeding expectations." TJ could see the genuine pride on Mikey's face.

"Well, I appreciate it, man," TJ said with genuine gratitude.

During dinner, TJ could not help but think about Mikey's answer: "We love to find people what they are looking for." His waitress was so happy when she saw him come to the table. It was like she could not wait to tell him they had his favorite cut of meat. TJ kept thinking she might be as happy about it as he was. "Nothing makes us happier," seemed to be the truth.

Mikey's team started determined to get the customer to what they needed or wanted, just maybe in a different way than they expected. "That could work," TJ thought. "Many times, we have a customer who wants to do something, but it's not allowed. If we can figure out the why behind the project request, maybe we can get them what they need, and they can leave satisfied. If we start with the expectation that we can and will find a solution that can get them to a yes, even if it's not their original ask, we can change the culture here."

The steak was good, but the best part . . . Light at the end of the tunnel!

CHAPTER 5
WHAT'S THE PLAN?

Early Saturday morning, TJ was back in his office. He had had a restless night of tossing and turning, thinking about that fantastic steak and the amazing culture of the restaurant that had brought it to him. As he came through the door of his office, the words on the whiteboard, WE LOOK FOR WAYS TO SAY NO, were screaming at him from across the room.

Still rubbing sleep from his eyes, TJ grabbed a fresh cup of coffee and sat down. He thought, man, this chair is the worst . . . The quiet of a Saturday morning alone sounded so good, but he wasn't going to be alone for long.

About ten minutes later, the door creaked open, and Jamie Lunds, the city's Human- Resources director, stepped inside. She was sharp, worked hard, and was one of TJ's most dependable allies. "Morning, TJ. You're here early. Don't you know it's Saturday?"

TJ gave her a tired smile. "Could say the same about you."

Jamie gave a side-eyed look at the whiteboard, saying thoughtfully . . . "We look for ways to say no." Walking over to the board, she continued, "What is all this about, Boss? It

A SOLUTION-FOCUSED CULTURE

looks like you have an idea you're working through. Want some help?"

TJ said, "I could sure use some!"

Trailing the words with her finger as she read, Jamie continued, "I really like this part. *Learn to get to what the customer really needs. We will help them find a solution that works for them and us.*"

TJ stood up and began to pace the floor across the office from her. "I've been thinking about how we've got a culture problem here in Clearview. It's not necessarily mismanagement, and our budget is in good shape; it's this instinct to shut down ideas before they even have a chance—not just internal ideas, but all ideas. It's like we are looking for the wrong in everything. There seems to be a regulatory culture that looks for a reason to say no and keeps moving farther away from yes."

Jamie, crossing her arms, said softly, almost to herself, "Regulatory culture . . . Yeah, I've seen it. Anytime someone brings something forward, boom, there's a million reasons why it won't work. I have often wondered why no one's asking how it *could* work. To be honest, when I first got here, I was always excited about new challenges.

I wanted to find solutions, but after time, you just get beat down."

"Exactly," TJ said, stepping up next to her. "I want to turn that way of thinking on its head. I had dinner at Sam's last night..."

Jamie interrupted excitedly, "They are the best. They will cook anything you want, any way you want, and their people are so happy! One time, my husband competed in a deep-sea fishing tournament. He came back with a big cobia. We had no idea how to cook it, so I called up there and asked for Mikey so I could ask him how to cook the fish. You know what he said?" Not letting TJ respond to the obviously rhetorical question, she continued, "He said, just come to dinner tonight and bring the fish with you. We will prepare it for you and your family. It was AMAZING! I think Mikey was as excited about cooking for us as my husband was with his tournament-winning fish."

TJ smiled. "Exactly! While I was there last night, I could not help but watch how happy everyone was working. I was thinking the same thing: the people at Sam's are happy because they actually get to help people get what they are looking for."

Jamie was following along and nodding as TJ continued, "We need to flip our way of doing business on its head. We need to get our people away from looking for the *regulation* that will help them say no, and move them toward looking for *resources* that support solutions."

At this point, TJ was really starting to get his mind around what they needed to do next. Not wanting him to slow down, Jamie said, "I see what you're saying. Keep going."

"I think the way to do that is through a framework that builds the right kind of culture—a culture that looks for legal, ethical, and moral ways around obstacles, one that helps people connect to the resources that will bring solutions, not only points out the regulations that could derail an idea."

Jamie looked intrigued. "I would love to help. Do you have something in mind?"

"I think we need to start by bringing everyone together," TJ said, frustrated as he tried to adjust his chair to sit back down at his desk. "We need an off-site meeting with all the department heads as soon as possible. We can use it as an opportunity to reset our thinking, to really hone in on what's going wrong with the culture and how we can change it."

Jamie thought for a moment. "I can help organize that. I bet we can use the conference room at the hotel downtown. They've got good facilities and a strong relationship with the city. It would take me about a week to set everything up. That should work out since we have the department head meeting on Monday morning and the city council workshop on Tuesday."

TJ's eyes brightened. "That sounds perfect. At the workshop, we will be working on updating the very outdated Strategic Plan and developing a mission statement."

Jamie said, "Yeah, I am working on the presentation you sent me through Christine on the existing plan and the framework for the SWOT analysis. That's why I came in today. I want to proof everything, but it's ready."

"OK, let's make it happen. These two weeks are going to be big for Clearview," TJ said confidently.

"Agreed, I will get on it Monday," Jamie said.

TJ nodded his head in approval. "For the off-site, we need more than just a meeting. I want to get input from the entire team. Let's start by conducting a survey this week. I want to ask our employees what's holding them back from doing their best work and what they think it would take to fix that."

Jamie raised an eyebrow. "Didn't I give you the results of that employee satisfaction survey we did last month?"

"You did," TJ replied, "but that survey was more about general feelings of job satisfaction. I am looking for something deeper. I want to know how our employees feel about their ability or lack of ability to solve problems. We need to know if they feel empowered. Do they believe they can be effective? If we're going to improve customer experience, we need to start by improving the employee experience."

Jamie leaned against the desk, her arms crossed, clearly thinking about what TJ said. "I couldn't agree more. You can't expect happy customers without happy employees. I also think you are on to something else: we need to connect with them on a different level and get their ideas on how to move forward."

They spent the next several hours hashing out details. On Monday, TJ would meet with each of the department heads to kick off the conversation. He wanted them to start thinking about examples of solution-focused approaches already happening within the organization. Despite a culture of "no," TJ had met plenty of employees, like Mary in the Engineering Department and Susan in Planning, who were eager to help customers but were bogged down by outdated policies and unnecessary bureaucracy.

He informed them that not only would they be at the Strategic Planning Workshop scheduled for Tuesday, but that the following week, they would be headed off-site to work on a plan for a new way of doing business in Clearview.

TJ would ask department heads to spend time getting to know all the challenges of the organization. He wanted them to work alongside employees and conduct informal surveys of the staff and the customers they served. TJ explained this to Jamie, saying, "I will need to make sure that everyone knows not to try to solve the problems they see; this is a fact-finding mission only. We will use all the information we are collecting to come up with a plan as a team."

"I think we've got a good strategy," Jamie said, scribbling notes as they spoke. "I'll start prepping the logistics for the off-site. In the meantime, you can hold that department head meeting and get everyone thinking about how we shift the focus from regulation to resources."

"That's the plan," TJ said, feeling a flicker of optimism. "We can't expect change overnight, but if we start getting people to think differently, we'll build momentum. We will create a culture where people look forward to coming to work because they know they're making a difference."

They stood there momentarily, staring at the board, now filled with ideas. The morning had turned into afternoon, and neither had noticed.

"We've got a long road ahead," TJ said, breaking the silence.

Jamie grinned. "Yeah, but at least now we have a map. On Monday, I will get to work on making arrangements for the off-site, but right now, I have to get to the house: I've got a date with my husband. And if I remember right, I heard Dawn say that Adeline has a game at 3:00 p.m. today, so you need to get going too!"

"Agreed, Monday starts a new way of doing business in Clearview. Have a great weekend," TJ said as he packed up his backpack.

Monday would be the first real test. He would challenge the department heads to think beyond their individual silos and embrace a new way of working together. They had to shift from a culture of "regulation" to one of "resources." It wasn't going to be easy, but TJ was ready. And with people like Jamie by his side, he believed they could turn Clearview into a city where both employees and citizens could thrive.

TJ smiled, wiping the whiteboard clean. He replaced, "WE LOOK FOR WAYS TO SAY NO," with a new phrase: "SOLUTION-FOCUSED."

CHAPTER 6
WHO HAS TIME FOR AN OFFSITE?

Monday morning came quickly for TJ, who found himself pacing around his office before the department head meeting. The time had come for him to challenge his leadership team to start thinking differently. It had been a long time since he was this excited to try a new idea. He had been observing the culture in Clearview for weeks and knew there was untapped potential in his staff, despite the ingrained habit of starting with "no."

Arriving early to the training room, TJ wrote on the large dry-erase board located at the front of the room, "**SOLUTION-FOCUSED**" in big, bold black letters. Shortly after, the department heads began to file into the room, TJ couldn't help but notice their varied expressions. As they found a seat, some looked curiously at the board and others seemed apprehensive, while at least one seemed downright indifferent. TJ decided to dive right in.

"Good morning, everyone. I appreciate you taking the time to meet today," TJ began. "I've been thinking a lot about our culture here in Clearview. As you know, I have spent some time in each department, meeting with staff and assessing the overall culture. The best way I can describe what I saw is like this: we have made regulation our identity."

As TJ looked around the room, he saw understanding on the face of the team.

"I want to challenge us all to approach things differently. We've been stuck in a mindset of focusing on why things *can't* work, rather than how they *can*. Starting today, I want us to look for examples of solution-focused approaches already happening within our departments. We've got great people like Mary in Engineering and Susan in Planning, who are eager to help customers, but they're bogged down by outdated policies and unnecessary bureaucracy."

TJ paused, scanning the room again for reactions. He saw a few nods.

"I'm asking each of you to spend this week informally surveying your teams and the public. Talk to them about what it would take to shift this mindset, to move from a culture of 'regulation' to one of finding solutions. I know this is a lot to ask," TJ conceded, "but we can't continue doing business the way we have. We have to evolve."

Kevin Ashton, the fire chief, was the first to speak. "I get what you're saying, TJ, and I think it's a good idea. But I've been here a long time, and I'm just not sure people will change. I'll talk to my team, but I'm not expecting miracles."

TJ appreciated Kevin's honesty. He knew the fire chief was nearing retirement and wouldn't be particularly excited about major changes this close to the end of his career. But he didn't need Kevin to be a cheerleader—just willing to try.

Next up was Carrie Smith, the Finance director. She adjusted her glasses, leaned forward, and declared, "I love the idea of shifting to a solution-focused culture. But to be honest, I'm a little worried about all this time away from the office for the off-site you're planning. I noticed on the calendar that we will be away for three whole days. We're all swamped, and I'm not sure we can afford to lose a week of productivity."

Walter Wooden, the Public Works director, chimed in, "Carrie's right. I'm all for making things better, but we've got a lot on our plates."

TJ smiled, appreciating their pragmatism. "I understand your concerns about time, but I believe that investing this week will pay off exponentially in the future. If we don't address our culture now, we'll keep running into the same problems over and over. We need this time away from the office to reset."

Darnell Williams, the Parks and Recreation director, leaned back in his chair and grinned. "I think it's great, TJ. I've already been talking to my team about how we can make our programs better for the community. I'll have to move some things around in my schedule, but I'm really looking forward to this off-site. We need to change the way we think."

TJ felt a wave of relief wash over him. Darnell's enthusiasm was contagious, and he watched it spread to the rest of the team.

Rick, the interim Planning director, spoke next. "I'm with you, Darnell. The Planning Department is drowning in old processes, and it's frustrating for everyone. I would love to connect my team to their purpose. They all want to help people and love to solve problems. I have never done an off-site and have no idea what to expect, but I know my team would love a fresh start!"

With the majority of the department heads on board, TJ felt confident in their next steps. "Alright, let's make it happen. Spend this week talking to your teams and the public. We'll meet at the off-site to discuss what you've learned." Wanting to make sure he set clear expectations, TJ reiterated, "Everyone needs to clear their schedule and let your assistants know that while in session, we won't be responding to email or text messages. We are going to be working on our new direction, and I want to make sure we are all concentrating on the task at hand."

A SOLUTION-FOCUSED CULTURE

Jamie, who had been sitting quietly until now, spoke up. "I've got the hotel conference room downtown lined up. They've been great partners with the city, and I figured it's the perfect spot. There is plenty of room, and it's quiet this time of year. I've also arranged for lunch to be catered by Mikey's every day."

TJ's eyebrows shot up. "Mikey's? That's perfect. It was the culture at Mikey's that sparked this whole idea."

Jamie gave a knowing smile. "I thought it was fitting. Not to mention, everyone loves their food, so it should keep morale high."

They wrapped up the meeting with a sense of cautious optimism. TJ knew there were still hurdles ahead, but it felt like they were moving in the right direction.

That afternoon, just as TJ was settling into his desk, there was a knock on his door. Sam Evans, one of the city councilmen, strode in without waiting for an invitation. Sam was a fixture in Clearview—sixty-seven years old, a grandfather of six, and a man who liked things to be the way they used to be. His family had been a part of Clearview for generations, with his father serving as a judge in the district for twenty-five years. Sam's family owned a significant amount of property in the city, much of it poorly maintained and a frequent subject of complaints.

TJ stood up to greet him. "Good afternoon, Mr. Evans. What can I do for you?"

Sam didn't waste time. "I have been talking with staff and hear you're planning some kind of off-site for the department heads. Do you really think it's a good idea to take them away from the office for a whole week? You have already caused some problems by firing one of the best employees this city has ever had." His voice rose as he spoke, "Don't you think this is a waste of time? What's the point, TJ? We've got plenty of issues to deal with right here in the city."

TJ took a deep breath. He had been expecting pushback

from Sam, whose reluctance to embrace change and long-standing family connections with Sarah were well-known. "I understand your concerns, Sam. But this off-site is about addressing the deeper issues that have been holding the city back. We need to change the way we approach our work if we're going to keep up with Clearview's growth."

Sam crossed his arms. "I've been here a long time, and things worked just fine the way they were. You want to change everything, but for what? The city's running fine. We don't need to reinvent the wheel."

TJ nodded, choosing his words carefully. "Sir, I'm not trying to change everything. I'm trying to make sure we're ready for the future. Clearview is growing, and with growth comes new challenges. We need to be proactive, not reactive."

Sam didn't look convinced, but TJ knew that changing how Sam felt about his approach to running the city would take time. "I'll keep an eye on it," Sam said before turning back toward the door. "It would serve you well to pay more attention to your staff when they suggest you shouldn't do things like this."

TJ, now beginning to fight back real frustration at the idea that someone on his team was trying to undermine the plans for change, stood up and walked over to shake Sam's hand before he left. "Thanks for stopping by, Sam. I do appreciate your take on this. I will certainly weigh the counsel of the team and will be looking forward to their continued input moving forward."

Sam shook his head, easing his tone some. "I am glad to hear that. Have a good day."

Less than an hour later, TJ received a phone call from Charles Cho, one of the newer council members. Charles was an interesting character—he had moved to Clearview after retiring from Space Experts, where he had worked as an aerospace engineer. His wife had fond memories of living near Clearview as a child, and when she became ill, Charles had moved them both back to the Gulf Coast. Despite his retirement, Charles wasn't one to sit idle, and he had run for city council in an effort to make a difference.

"Hey, TJ, I wanted to give you a heads-up," Charles said, his voice full of energy. "I've got some news. There's a potential manufacturing company looking at setting up shop here in Clearview. It's a big deal, and I want to make sure we're ready."

TJ's ears perked up. "That's great news, Charles. What do you need from us?"

"Just make sure the staff is prepared to handle it. This could be a big opportunity for the city, and I want to be sure we've got the right people in place to make it happen."

TJ smiled. "That's exactly what we have been working on. We are headed to a multi-day off-site meeting next week to continue develop-ing a plan to improve the way we do business. Where are they looking to go?"

Charles responded, "Of course, this is not public yet, but they want to fill the old shopping center on Evans Parkway."

Familiar with the location and knowing immediately that

it was not well suited for manufacturing and the zoning would not be a good fit, TJ replied, "That's an interesting pick for a location."

Charles, sensing something was up, said, "Now, TJ, this is a big deal for us. They can bring a lot of high-paying jobs. We were on the shortlist for another company to come to Clearview last year, but they went to the next county because we were too difficult to deal with. I told these guys not to worry; that's why you are here . . . They don't need to worry, do they?"

TJ responded, trying to sound confident: "I am looking forward to working with them. This is just the kind of thing we will be discussing at our off-site next week. Please email me their contact information, and we will get it worked out."

"Glad to hear it, TJ. Let's make this happen," Charles said before hanging up.

TJ sat back in that miserable chair and thought, "It's time to go home; tomorrow, we define the mission!"

CHAPTER 7
ON A MISSION!

The sun cut through the fog early Tuesday morning as TJ made his way into the Clearview City Council chambers, feeling the full weight of the day ahead. Today, he had called a workshop meeting with the city council and department heads to tackle a critical task—developing a mission statement for Clearview. In the weeks since his arrival, TJ had observed the city's culture and operations and realized that the city lacked a clear, unifying purpose. Without a defined mission, it was easy for departments to operate in silos, each with their own goals and strategies, sometimes working against each other. This was the way Clearview had operated for the last fifty years.

By 8:30 a.m., TJ was seated at his place on the dais, ready for what he knew would be a long but important session. The mayor, Richard Whitmore, a retired army captain who had served in various leadership roles during his military career, was already there drinking coffee with Councilman Cho. The men stood next to the table of refreshments, discussing how they thought the day would go. Both seemed optimistic.

"This is a good idea, TJ," Mr. Cho said as he walked up to his seat.

A SOLUTION-FOCUSED CULTURE

Over the next few minutes, the rest of the council and department heads began to file in, their faces a mix of curiosity and mild apprehension. Jamie worked to set up audio and video for the day while Walter and Mr. Evans shared a conversation by the door. TJ thought to himself, "I need to get this right today.

As the clock struck 9:00 a.m., Mayor Whitmore called the meeting to order. After going through the typical motions of opening a public meeting, the group stood for a prayer and said the Pledge of Allegiance.

"This isn't a typical meeting," Mayor Whitmore said. "Today is about setting a course for the city's future. We only have one item for discussion, so TJ, the floor is yours."

"Thank you all for coming," TJ began, walking over to the podium. I've asked the mayor to call this workshop because we need to develop a mission statement for the city. Right now, we're operating without a clear guide. Over the last few weeks, I visited the different departments in the city to see what everyone does, what resources they need, and what we can do better. The piece that seemed to be missing in every department was a unified, well-defined mission."

"TJ, are you saying people don't know what they are doing?" Council Member Harris said in obvious surprise. "Do you really think a catchphrase will fix that?"

TJ, regaining the floor, said, "Ms. Harris, the employees are very competent, qualified, and ready to do their jobs. A mission statement is more than just a few words on a website—it's the backbone of every decision we make. It's not that they lack technical skills; it's that they, or I should say we, need a way to be reminded of the bigger picture."

The mayor nodded in agreement, his military background lending itself naturally to understanding the importance of clear, strategic directives. "In the army, we always had a mission," he said, his gravelly voice commanding attention. "Without one, people don't know where they're supposed to go or what they're supposed to do when the plan falls apart. You can't win a battle without a mission."

TJ, excited that there was solid participation this early, said, "That's right, Mayor Whitmore. Every organization needs to understand its mission. However, to continue with that concept, it's important not only to define the mission but boil it down to a single statement that sums up the organization's purpose. It should define our 'why.'"

The city clerk, Irene Grant, an experienced, highly educated woman in her late sixties who was always eager to contribute, chimed in. "It becomes the policy when no other policy exists. A good mission statement is what ties everything together and gives us direction when we're faced with tough choices."

"Exactly," TJ exclaimed.

Council Member Cho spoke up next. "In my time at Space Experts, we had a clear mission statement. It was the thing that united all departments, from engineering to HR. It gave everyone a sense of purpose. 'Get There First and Safe,' that was our mission statement!" he said with pride. "That very simple statement is what helped me argue for more funding or agree to additional safety protocols, because I knew that my job was to get us there first and safe."

TJ, loving Councilman Cho's energy, said, "Precisely! Now, if everyone can open their binders, Jamie will give us a brief overview of where we are on the current Strategic Plan."

Jamie, with confidence, replaced TJ at the podium and started. "Three years ago, the city council completed a strengths, weaknesses, opportunities, and threats (SWOT) analysis. You all received a copy of this analysis with the invitation to this meeting, and it is in the binder in front of you. I am hopeful you have had a chance to review it."

The mayor spoke up, "It seemed to me that the information was still relevant. I do think that some of the pressing issues have changed, but for the most part, I think the con-

A SOLUTION-FOCUSED CULTURE

dition of the city is either the same or worse than it was the day we completed this."

"That's right. That is also why I thought it was a waste of time then and still is today," Sam Evans chimed in somewhat condescendingly.

Wanting to protect his team and ensure the meeting stayed on track, TJ spoke up: "Councilman Evans, I understand that sentiment. Unfortunately, it's not uncommon for this type of work to be done well but never really acted on. Rest assured, that is why I am here. It won't happen again." Nodding to Jamie, TJ encouraged, "Jamie, proceed."

"I want to start by looking at the SWOT analysis you all did a couple of years back," Jamie said, clicking a button on the projector to display the information on the screen behind her. "This gives us a foundation—a snapshot of where we were. I think we can use this to help shape our new mission."

For the next thirty minutes, the group reviewed the strengths, weaknesses, opportunities, and threats laid out in the analysis. Some strengths were obvious: Clearview had a strong sense of community, a low crime rate, and a growing population. But there were weaknesses too. The regulatory mindset, which had dominated Clearview for years, had alienated developers, slowed business growth, and frustrated residents.

TJ pointed to the list of opportunities. "Here's where I think we have the most potential. Clearview is growing. We're on the cusp of some big things. We have new businesses interested in coming here. We're located near a major military base, and we're attractive to families who want a safe, welcoming place to live. But none of this will matter if we don't get our internal culture right and clarify our purpose."

Mayor Whitmore leaned back in his chair, rubbing his chin. "So we need to figure out how to turn these opportunities into strengths and how to address the weaknesses head-on."

TJ nodded. "Exactly. And to do that, we need a clear mission statement, something that reflects not only what we do but why we do it. Something that gives our employees, our residents, and our businesses a sense of who we are as a city."

Council member Kim Bolder, who had been relatively quiet up until this point, spoke up. "But what do we actually want Clearview to be? We have all these pieces in place, but what's our overarching goal? What's our city's identity?"

"That's what we need to define," Jamie said. "And I think we can do it by answering a simple question: What kind of city do we want Clearview to be in the future? When people think of Clearview, what do we want them to say?"

The group spent the next several hours brainstorming, going back and forth between ideas. TJ was really encouraged by the participation of not only the council but also his team. At first, the suggestions were vague: "A great place to live," "A city that works for everyone," "A place for opportunity." But slowly, with input from both the council members and department heads, the ideas began to coalesce into something more concrete.

Councilman Cho, drawing from his experience in engineering, stressed the need for precision. "We need something measurable, something that gives people a clear idea of what success looks like."

The mayor nodded. "We need to focus on three key things: making Clearview a great place to live, a great place to work, and a great place to play."

TJ, noticing that Carrie, the finance director, had something to say, said, "Carrie, what are you thinking."

"Well," she said somewhat reservedly, "I think we're getting somewhere. 'Live, work, and play.' That's the core of what we're trying to achieve, isn't it? We want people to come here because it's the best place to raise a family, start a business, and enjoy life."

Rick, the interim Planning director, said, "I like it! That's why I am here."

By noon, after several rounds of discussion and revisions, they had the final version of the mission statement:

"Making Clearview the Best Place to Live, Work, and Play."

The room was quiet for a moment as everyone took it in. Then, slowly, heads began to nod in agreement.

The mayor was the first to speak. "That's it. That's what we're about."

Councilman Cho agreed. "It's minimal, but it says everything we need to say. It's aspirational, but it's also something we can work toward every day."

TJ exhaled, feeling a sense of relief wash over him. They had done it. They had a mission statement that not only captured the city's purpose but also gave them a clear direction for the future. He glanced at the clock. It had been a four-hour session, but it had been worth it.

"I think we've got it," TJ said. "This is going to be the foundation for everything we do moving forward. But this is just the beginning. I'm working with the department heads to evaluate where we are right now, with surveys, face-to-face meetings, and conversations with the public. We'll need to update our strategic plan in a couple of months after we get a better handle on our current operations."

The mayor, looking to see if anyone else had a comment, said, "Meeting adjourned!"

As the meeting wrapped up, TJ thanked everyone for their participation and invited them to enjoy the lunch catered by Mikey's before they left. There was a sense of unity in the room that hadn't been there before. The mission statement wasn't just words on paper—it was something they had all created together, something they believed in.

When the council adjourned, TJ made his way back to his office. As he walked through the hallways, he couldn't help but feel hopeful. Today had been a big step in the right direction.

Back in his office, Christine, his ever-reliable assistant, was waiting for him. She grinned when she saw him walk in. "So, I watched the meeting on social media. I'm curious to see what you think about it . . . sooo, how'd it go, Boss?"

TJ chuckled, collapsing into his chair. "It went well, Christine. We've got ourselves a mission statement."

Christine raised an eyebrow, saying, "'Making Clearview the Best Place to Live, Work, and Play.'" She nodded thoughtfully. "I like it. It's got a nice ring to it."

"Yeah, I think it's going to be the thing that pulls us all together," TJ said.

Before they could dive into the next challenge on his desk, Jamie poked her head into the office. "TJ, you have a minute?"

"Sure, come on in," he said, waving her in.

Jamie walked in with her notebook in hand. "I wanted to strategize about the off-site and how we're going to push the new mission statement out to the employees and the public."

TJ nodded. "That's exactly what we need to be thinking

about. We've got the statement, but now we need to make sure it's more than just words. We need to make it part of the culture."

For the next few days, TJ, Jamie, and Christine met multiple times. They worked through the logistics of getting the mission statement out to the employees and the public. The three talked about newsletters, website updates, and even video messages from the mayor and council. It was going to be a lot of work, but TJ felt energized by the progress they had made.

As the week stretched on, TJ found himself feeling more optimistic than he had since coming to Clearview. The city was beginning to move in the right direction. They had a mission, and soon, they would have the culture to match it.

By the end of the week, everything was in place for the three-day off-site. The hotel was booked, Mikey's was ready to cater, and the department heads had spent the week gathering insights from their teams. TJ felt optimistic. He knew the off-site wouldn't solve everything overnight, but it was a step in the right direction.

As he packed up for the weekend, TJ allowed himself a rare moment of satisfaction. The future of Clearview might still be uncertain, but for the first time, he felt like they were actively shaping it rather than simply reacting to it.

CHAPTER 8
LAYING THE GROUNDWORK

It was early Monday morning when TJ arrived at the hotel conference room, ready to kick off the off-site. Arriving there an hour early, he was nervous but determined. This was the first step toward reshaping Clearview's culture, and although the task seemed daunting, TJ was ready to lead the charge. His mind was racing with ideas as he set up the room, preparing for the day ahead.

As he laid out the materials, he noticed Walter Wooden walking through the door, balancing a large box of doughnuts and two jugs of coffee.

"Morning," Walter greeted him with a sheepish smile. "Brought some fuel for the team."

TJ smiled back. "Thanks, man, you are here early."

"Yeah," Walter said, glancing around the empty room. "I was actually hoping to catch you before everyone else got here." He hesitated for a moment, then gestured for TJ to step aside.

Curious, TJ nodded and followed him. Once they were out of earshot of the entrance, Walter handed him a coffee. Rubbing his beard, he spoke quietly. "Look, man, I owe you an apology. I, uh, might have talked to Sam Evans last week about this whole off-site thing."

TJ tried to fix the look he knew was on his face, but he was unsure where this was going. "Go on."

Walter sighed. "I didn't mean any harm—well, maybe I did at first. I ran into him at the store during lunch on the day the off-site came up, and we got to talking about how things were going. I told him I wasn't sure if this off-site was the best use of our time. You know how Sam is; he's not one for change, and I guess I was just venting. I think the problem for me is, if I admit that the things you are trying to do are what we need, then my life's work seems like a failure. I mean, I have been here for so long that I feel like this place is a part of me. I acted out of fear. I was afraid these changes would taint my legacy; if people see things could've been better, they will think less of me."

Observing Walter, the furrow of his brow, and the tightness around his eyes, TJ responded immediately. "Walter, I know that all this change can be difficult and that when we are talking about changing systems you had a part in developing, it can seem like an attack on your legacy. It is important you know that's not the case. The work you did over the years kept the city moving forward. What we are doing now is just the next step in that process. I really don't want to have to try to do this without you on the team. You are an influential leader here, and people want to follow you. People like Councilman Evans look to you for reassurance that we are moving in the right direction."

"I know you are right," Walter said. "I have been thinking about it all weekend, and I realized that this off-site might be exactly what we need. That's why I'm here early. I want to start the week off right and let you know I'm all in. Whatever you need from me, I'm ready."

Walter had been with the city for over two decades, and his support mattered. Hearing his shift in attitude made TJ feel like the week might just go smoother than expected. "I appreciate that, Walter. It means a lot that you're on board. We're going to get a lot done this week, and I'm glad you'll be part of it." Patting him on the back, TJ went on, "From now on, if you have any concerns with what we are doing, promise me you will come to me and talk about it. We can grab lunch or get some coffee and work through whatever is on your mind."

"Deal," Walter answered, the tightness in his face now relaxed.

They shook hands, and as other department heads began trickling in, TJ's nerves started to buzz again. He had conducted these off-sites dozens of times and understood that execution was everything. He knew from experience that the success of the next few days would depend on how well the team embraced the process.

Once everyone settled in, TJ moved to the large notepad on the easel at the front of the room. In bold letters, he wrote: **Solution-Focused Culture.** He underlined it twice and then turned to face the team.

"This," he said, pointing to the words on the page, "is what we're here to develop."

He then wrote underneath it: *"Making Clearview the Best Place to Live, Work, and Play."*

"And this," he emphasized, "is why we are going to be successful in making it happen."

A few heads nodded, but there were still some uncertain faces in the room. TJ decided to start with someone he knew had fully embraced the idea. Feeling like he and Walter were in a good place after their earlier conversation, TJ asked him to go first.

"Walter, why don't you start us off this morning? What did you find in your talks with the team?" TJ said, pulling a page from the notepad and sticking it to the wall.

Walter straightened up in his chair. "I spent some time

talking to the engineers, and they had a few suggestions. One that stood out was the idea of creating a quick reference guide for residents and developers who are filling out development order applications. Right now, it's a complicated process, and people get frustrated because they don't know what they're supposed to do. This guide could make things a lot smoother."

TJ began his list by writing, "*Quick-reference guides.*" He liked the practicality of the idea but really wanted to explore something more related to culture.

Noticing the rest of the team nodding, Walter was gaining confidence. He continued, "One of the things that really stood out to me was that I think the team is sometimes confused about what we . . . or I should say you and the council want."

TJ, loving the openness so early in the process, said, "Tease that out for me a little bit, Walter. What do you mean?"

"Well, I think that sometimes they are unclear on when it is OK to say no and when it is OK to suggest changes." Walter continued with a little bit of apprehension. "I mean, a good example is, the other day, we had an application for a new fast-food restaurant. The site plan was pretty good, but the drive-through was laid out so that the lights from cars in the queue would be pointing into the apartment on the property next door. It is typically our practice not to allow that because it creates a problem for the adjacent property, but the code is not really clear that it's not allowed or what the rule is. Since this is a friend of Councilwoman Bolder, the team was very concerned about giving any suggestions and also concerned that when they denied it, they would be in trouble. They feel like they don't know what the expectation is, so they just take a hard line and get prepared to defend it."

Darnell jumped in. "They need a backstop."

The room looked at him, somewhat confused. Carrie said, "A backstop? At a fast-food restaurant?"

Kevin laughed, "Yeah, man, you may want to stick to bats

and balls and let the engineers handle the sight design. How about you and me just do our thing and eat there when it's built?"

Everyone laughed at the playful banter.

"Not an actual backstop," Darnell said, laughing himself, "but a good burger does sound good." Now, even TJ was laughing as Darnell continued, "I am saying, like on a baseball field, behind the plate, there is a backstop. Nothing gets by it. It's like a line in the sand that says no matter how hard you throw the ball, it will stop here. If they had a backstop, they would know that nothing gets past it." Looking around to see if the team was getting it, he continued, "OK, let me put it this way: on the football field, there are lines. These lines draw a box around the field of play. Inside the box, the players can do all sorts of things to get to the end zone, but outside the lines is out of bounds. Inside the box, they can run the ball, pass the ball, pitch it, and even kick it.

The quarterback starts with a play from the coach, but sometimes the defense gives you something to make that play not work, so you have to make a change. As long as you stay inside the box and move the ball forward, the coach will be happy. We need to give them a box," Darnell said confidently.

"Man, that is a lot of sports analogies," Jamie said with a smile. "I hate sports. I just don't get them," she said, poking Darnell a little.

"Yeah, that is a lot of sports, but I think we can work with it," TJ said, loving the energy and camaraderie in the room. "Let's use the term *Give them a box* for our notes. No one will forget that," TJ said, smiling. Then he continued, "Jamie, tell us what you discovered while surveying your team and the customers. What can we do to be more solution focused?"

Jamie sat up straighter in her chair. "Well, I spent a good bit of time talking to our employees and a few residents who've had to deal with the city recently. I found that a lot of their frustration comes from the fact that we have these rigid policies that don't allow us to be flexible, even when flexibility would benefit the customer and the city. For example, with HR, we have some outdated processes that slow everything down. My team wants to help more, but we're stuck following procedures that no longer make sense."

Frank interjected, "Jamie, I think you are on to something here. The other day I was talking to your team about a new hire. As everyone knows, it's hard to find and hire good police officers right now; I had a great one that we wanted to offer the job to, but by the time all the paperwork got done and we called, he had taken another job." The frustration was clear on the police chief's face as he continued, "That kills the morale of my team. They are overwhelmed with all the overtime and struggle not to get discouraged."

Jamie responded, "Yeah when I talked to them later that day, they were telling me that they had a bunch of good ideas on how to fix the paperwork problems but don't feel like it's their place to do it. The more we talked, the more I started to realize that some of the frustrating red tape is from the policy decisions made right here with this team. No one came right out and said it, but it was obvious that they were frustrated. We set policy without talking to them first. To rub salt in the wound, we turn around and get after them for it not working well."

Frank concurred, "I got the same sense. I was going to suggest we get them to give us feedback on the current process."

TJ scribbled on his notepad as Jamie spoke, jotting down key points. "*Rigid policies*," he repeated aloud as he wrote. "*Lack of flexibility. Ask the subject matter experts.*"

"And it's not just internal issues," Jamie continued. "We heard from some residents that they get shuffled between departments, each one saying they can't help because it's not their job. That's something we need to address." Pausing for a moment, then remembering the name of a book she read, she said, "A couple of years ago, I read a book by Patrick Lencioni called *Silos, Politics and Turf Wars*. It talked about this exact thing. I think over the years, we have turned into a collection of silos."

TJ nodded, adding *Departmental silos* to the list. "Thanks, Jamie. This is good insight. I saw some of the same things on my department visits."

After a brief pause, TJ suggested a break so everyone could return phone calls, use the restroom, and clear their heads before continuing. While they were outside, TJ returned a call he had been avoiding. It was another complaint. As he worked through the issue, he took a moment to review the growing list of challenges and ideas on the board. It was starting to come together, but there was still a lot of work to do.

When they reconvened, TJ turned next to Kevin Ashton, the fire chief, who had expressed some initial reluctance. "Kevin, how about you? What did you learn?"

Kevin took a deep breath before speaking. "I admit I was a little skeptical at first, but I actually had some great conversations with my guys. I really enjoyed it. They're surprisingly on board with the idea of changing the way we do business. One of my fire inspectors had a pretty cool idea."

TJ, loving this new level of buy-in from the fire chief, said, "What was it?"

Kevin continued, "Well, in the fire service, we are very big about our identity. As you know, we have multiple stations. Each one has its own logo and even its own identity. Jonny, that's the inspector's name, came from the coast guard. He said their motto is *'Semper Paratus,'* which translates to 'Always Ready.' He said that even though each station had its own identity, no matter where you are, you know the mission or purpose is to be 'always ready.' He said we need a rallying cry to ensure we all pull in the same direction. I get that we just approved the mission statement, but I think it is more like an internal motto."

"That's good." TJ nodded.

"Right?" Kevin said, "I think we really need to make that a part of this process—something we can all get behind. When we do it, we need to make sure we connect it to what each department does."

Feeling a sense of encouragement that Kevin was truly excited about something in the process, TJ wrote on the notepad, *Rallying cry to connect the employees to our purpose.*

Kevin continued, "I have one more thing that came up . . . if I may?"

TJ insisted, "Of course. What else did you find?"

"We tend to follow protocol to the letter, even when unnecessary. We've had a few situations where a little common sense could have made things easier for both us and the residents, but we stuck to the book. I am not talking about when we are fighting fires. I mean, like denying a public appearance during Fire Safety Week because of a missed request deadline or advising a better way to do something on an inspection. That's something we think we need to work on. I think it all gets back to Walter's point about guidelines." Kevin looked around, feeling accomplished.

TJ made a note. "Good—*More discretion where it makes sense*. Anything else?"

Kevin added, "Yeah, they also feel like they're not always empowered to make decisions on the spot. They have to run everything up the chain, which slows things down."

Ability to solve problems, TJ wrote on the board. "Thanks, Kevin."

Next up was Frank Cannon, the police chief, who had been with the department for over a decade. As always, he spoke candidly.

"My team's biggest issue is that they feel like the past is still following them. We've had some rough years with public perception, and even though we've made a lot of progress, it seems like people still see us the way we were five or six years ago. It's hard to move forward when the community doesn't recognize the changes we've already made. We need help rebuilding trust."

TJ paused before writing *Public perception* on the board. "That's a tough one, Frank. But it's something we can definitely work on. Building trust takes time, but we can start by being more transparent and proactive."

Carrie interjected, "Frank, do you think the perception is really as bad as you think it is, or maybe it's just that your team believes that, so they have it—" she paused while thinking

"—hanging over their heads. I am just thinking. It's been a long time since I heard anyone refer to our police department with a negative tone. The only exception is the officers when they talk about how they *feel* the people see them."

"Maybe . . . I hadn't really thought of that," Frank considered.

TJ took the opportunity to jump in, "I think Carrie is on to something. A colleague of mine in the consulting business once shared that he worked with an organization that wasn't nearly as bad as they believed themselves to be. He told me that if they could let go of the past, they'd be much happier and more successful moving forward. I think we need to really work on connecting your team to the new identity. You have made great strides; we need to promote that internally as well as to the public."

While TJ walked back over to the board to write, *Encourage the team to see how great they are*, Frank said, "I think there is some truth to that. It's like they are defeated. If they can see how great they are, it will change the way they feel about themselves and the city."

Then Carrie recalled, "I had some interesting conversations with my staff. One story stuck out in particular. A resident came in last week to set up water service for their new house, and it took them three trips and two days to get it done. They were frustrated and angry, and frankly, I don't blame them. Our process is too convoluted."

TJ scribbled, *Complex processes* and *Customer frustration* on his notepad.

She continued, "When the technician returned from turning on the water, I heard him talking to some of the ladies up front. He said that when he is made to go to places like that and people treat him that way, he hates coming to work and feels that he looks stupid and incompetent. I felt bad for him, but what he and Angie, the billing clerk, talked about next was eye-opening. Angie said that you would think they would trust the people doing the job when it comes to setting up the systems for this stuff. We could get it done and keep people happy, but, no, we have to stick to these antiquated systems, and now the new guy is over here wanting us to make people happy. If that is what he wants, then he should let us do it!" Carrie continued, "The thing that stuck out to me was that the people working with the systems are the subject matter experts;

they are the ones best suited to solve many of these problems."

TJ said, "I think you are right. To use Darnell's analogy, once the box is in place, they can help develop the solutions."

Carrie sighed. "We've gotten so used to doing things a certain way that we've stopped questioning whether it still makes sense. I think we can do better."

"Agreed," TJ said, appreciating her honesty. He put a star by the term *subject matter experts*.

He then turned to Rick, who had been quiet most of the morning. "Rick, what did you learn from your team? I am really interested in your perspective since you are new to the team."

Rick, the interim Planning director, jumped right in. "I agree with Walter. There are *definitely* things we can do to help customers navigate our processes more easily. But I also heard from my team about some frustrations with internal services, particularly the network. They're constantly waiting for IT to get things done, and it's slowing them down. Even when the IT guys know what needs to happen, they can't get it done because they're waiting on another department." Rick was looking around and continued, "Bobby over in Business Tax Receipts also has some ideas on reducing the number of forms we use."

"OK, this sounds a little bit like more of the same. Employees are not empowered to make decisions even when they know the answer," TJ said as he wrote, *Internal service frustrations*.

By the time the clock struck noon, the board was filled with key phrases, each representing a challenge or opportunity. Lunch from Mikey's arrived, and the team took a break, enjoying lighthearted conversation over sandwiches and chips. The mood was noticeably more relaxed, and TJ felt a glimmer of hope. Maybe they really could turn things around.

After lunch, TJ gathered the group back together and

stood before the board. "Alright, let's break this down. We've gathered a lot of information this morning, and now we need to start categorizing it."

The team worked together, sorting the points into categories: Customer Experience, Internal Processes, Public Perception, and Employee Empowerment. As they moved through the topics, conversations sparked about how to address each challenge. Ideas flowed more freely than TJ had anticipated, and for the first time, he saw a true team effort emerging.

They took one last break before the final session of the day. During this final session TJ planned to introduce the potential manufacturing plant that Councilman Cho had mentioned.

When everyone returned, TJ got everyone's attention. "Tomorrow, we will begin to work through this list and develop a plan to address the different items. Before we wrap up, there's something we need to discuss that will be critical for the future of Clearview."

He outlined the details of the new manufacturing company considering moving to town. "This is a huge opportunity for us, but there are some challenges. The proposed location isn't ideal, and the zoning doesn't fit the use. That said, landing this factory could provide a significant economic stimulus for our community. I want to use the time we have together on this off-site to develop a new way of doing business that will make projects like this successful."

Then he exclaimed, "Great work today, team! Get some sleep," encouraged by the day.

CHAPTER 9
VALUES MATTER

The sun was barely up when TJ Strong stepped into the hotel conference room on the second day of Clearview's off-site meeting. As he closed the door behind him, he paused to look around the space, the faint smell of coffee lingering in the air from the morning brew. The room was quiet, but there was an undeniable energy that hung in the air—a sense of purpose that hadn't been there the day before.

The previous day had gone better than he had hoped. The team had opened up about the challenges they faced and started identifying the building blocks for change. Today, though, was the day they would begin to shape those ideas into something tangible, something that could drive the city toward a new, solution-focused culture. TJ had been thinking about it all night, unable to sleep as he considered the direction they should take.

As he adjusted the notepad on the easel and flipped through the pages from the day before, the door creaked open, and Jamie walked in, her usual upbeat energy already radiating. She held two coffees and handed one to TJ with a smile.

A SOLUTION-FOCUSED CULTURE

"Good morning, TJ. I figured I would find you here early. How are you feeling after yesterday?" she asked, settling into one of the chairs.

"I'm feeling good, actually, really good," TJ replied, pausing to blow on his coffee in an attempt to cool it a little. "Yesterday went better than expected. Everyone seemed to open up, and the ideas we collected were solid. And today, we get to try to figure out how to make sense of it all."

Jamie nodded. "I was thinking the same thing. We covered a lot of ground, but it's a bit scattered. What direction do you want to take today?"

TJ paused for a moment, choosing his words carefully. "I've been thinking about it all night. We need to start by prioritizing the categories we came up with yesterday into something we can work with. Once we do that, I think it'll be easier to move forward."

Just as they started discussing the different points from the previous day, Darnell walked in. "Morning, you two," he said with a grin. "Am I interrupting some early-morning strategy?"

"Not at all," TJ said, waving him over. "We were just talking about how to organize everything from yesterday."

Darnell nodded. "Yeah, we covered a lot. Feels like we're getting somewhere."

TJ walked over to the wall, where yesterday's sticky notes were still hanging. He pulled off the one that said *Build a box* in big, bold letters and held it up. "I think we start here," he said.

Jamie groaned playfully. "Oh no, not another sports example. I told you yesterday, TJ—I don't do sports."

They all laughed, the kind of easy laughter that came when you started to see the team dynamic taking shape. As they were still chuckling, Frank Cannon, the police chief, walked in, looking more relaxed than the day before.

"Did the party start without me?" Frank joked, taking a seat at the table.

"Kind of," Darnell replied, grinning. "TJ was just about to take us down the sports rabbit hole again."

Frank chuckled. "I'm OK with it. Actually, over dinner last night, I was talking with my wife, Lisa, about the whole backstop and box thing described. You know she played softball in college, right? Anyway, she said, 'You guys are really talking about core values. That's what the backstop is—it's about having something solid behind you that drives decisions.'"

TJ smiled and wrote *Establish core values* on the whiteboard. "I think Lisa hit the nail on the head. That's exactly what we need to do today—establish the core values that will guide us."

The rest of the department heads trickled in one by one, and soon, the room was filled with a quiet buzz of anticipation. As the last of the team took their seats, TJ stood up and addressed them all.

"Alright, everyone, here's the plan for today," TJ began. "Yesterday, we talked about the challenges we face and the changes we must make. Darnell spoke about the need for us to give a big box for our employees to work within. We have been thinking about how to do that and have decided we need to establish our core values—the foundation for everything we do moving forward. We have our mission statement, and now these values will provide the guiding framework for our decisions, shape our culture, and help to begin *Making Clearview the Best Place to Live, Work, and Play*."

Jamie said, "For this to work, we need the input of our employees. I have a copy of the electronic surveys we did. I think that some of the questions there will help us see what values are important to them."

TJ replied, "That is an excellent idea. Before we finalize the definitions, we can put together a team to help us define each value in a way that will connect to the whole organization. Let's get started!"

Nearly instantaneously, the whole team leaned forward, ready to dig in.

"Let's start with integrity," Frank said.

"I like it," TJ said as he nodded to Frank to continue. "What does this mean to us as a city?"

Frank spoke first. "Integrity is about doing the right thing, even when no one's watching. We've had our struggles in the police department with public perception, but we've always tried to operate with integrity. It's the cornerstone of trust."

Darnell nodded in agreement. "Without integrity, none of the other values matter. We need to set the example for the community."

TJ added *Integrity* to the board and wrote, *Upholding the highest standards of honesty and ethics in everything we do.*

Next, Jamie suggested transparency. "We've talked a lot about the frustration employees feel when they don't know what's going on. We need to be open with our staff and the public. If we communicate clearly, we can avoid a lot of the problems we're facing now."

Carrie, the Finance director, chimed in. "Yes, and transparency isn't just about communication. It's about being honest, even when it's difficult. If we're transparent, we'll build trust with the community, especially when it comes to how we spend taxpayer dollars."

TJ wrote *Transparency* on the board, adding, *Open and honest communication with our employees and community.*

The next value came naturally: respect. "I've seen a lack of respect in some of our departments," Darnell admitted. "We need to do better, not just with the public, but with each other."

Jamie agreed. "Respect isn't just about being polite. It's about valuing each person, even when we don't feel like it. I had a boss tell me one time, 'We will treat people with more respect than they deserve.' If we respect our team members and the residents we serve, it'll transform how we interact."

TJ added *Respect* to the board: *Showing respect for each other and the public.*

Walter, the Public Works director, spoke up. "Now I've been guilty of this in the past. Sometimes it's easier to blame the system or point fingers. But we need to take responsibility for our actions. If something goes wrong, we own it and we fix it. I think the next value should be accountability."

Everyone agreed, and TJ wrote *Accountability* on the board, adding, *Taking responsibility for our actions and outcomes.*

"This city's growing fast," Carrie said. "If we keep doing things the way we always have, we'll fall behind. We need to embrace new ideas, even if they're uncomfortable. What would be a good way to articulate a value that will help us stay ahead of all this growth and the challenges it brings while embracing new ideas?"

Rick jumped in. "What about innovative?"

Chief Aston nodded. "In my department, innovation can mean life or death. We've got to be open to new approaches if we're going to meet the challenges of a growing city."

A SOLUTION-FOCUSED CULTURE

TJ wrote *Innovation* on the board, adding, *Embracing new ideas and approaches to meet the challenges of a growing city.*

Before they knew it, the clock struck 10:30, and TJ called for a morning break. The team stood, stretching and grabbing fresh coffee before settling back into their seats.

Watching everyone enjoying each other's company during the break gave Walter an idea for the next value. Once everyone was seated, he moved over to the notepad and wrote *Teamwork.*

"I know that for years we have had siloed departments," Walter said. "That has to change. We need to work together—both within the city and with our community partners."

Darnell grinned. "You know I love teamwork. If we're going to accomplish anything, we need to be on the same page."

Jamie nodded. "We're stronger when we work together. We each bring something different to the table, and we need to leverage that."

TJ added to the word *Teamwork* Walter had written on the board: *Working together as a team, both within the city and with our community partners.*

After some discussion of whether or not another value was needed, Carrie said, "I think we need one more. I think we need to put *selflessness* as a value we pursue."

"This one's important," TJ said. "We're here to serve the public, and that means putting their needs ahead of our own."

Carrie agreed. "Selflessness is about treating people well. Whether it's a resident trying to set up water service or a business applying for permits, we need to go the extra mile to help."

TJ added *Selflessness* to the board: *Putting the customer first and treating others well.*

As they looked at the list of core values on the board,

Darnell suddenly chuckled. "Hey, you guys notice something?"

The team looked at him, confused.

"Look at the first letters of each value," Darnell said, pointing at the board. "Integrity, transparency, respect, accountability, innovation, teamwork, selflessness. If we move it around a little, it spells out *TRAITS*."

Jamie laughed. "I hate sports, but I love this! We're looking for the right 'TRAITS' in the people we hire and develop."

The rest of the team grinned, realizing that the acronym wasn't just a coincidence—it was exactly what they were aiming for: the right traits in their leadership and their employees.

After the late-day refreshment break, the team reconvened, feeling energized by their progress. TJ stood at the front of the room, beaming.

"You guys did some amazing work today," he said. "We've established our core values, and I think they will transform how we operate. Now, let's take the last hour to draw a direct connection between the mission statement and the core values."

The room buzzed with ideas as the team began discussing how the city's mission statement connected to each of the values and all of the individual departments' responsibilities. For each department, the team developed clear and concise ways to relay the information to the staff.

Looking around the room, TJ felt a sense of pride. They had done it. They had laid the foundation for a solution-focused culture grounded in core values and a clear mission. Now, the real work would begin, but TJ was confident they were ready for the challenge.

"We did it," TJ said, smiling at his team. "Let's make tomorrow the best day of this off-site!"

CHAPTER 10
RALLYING FOR A NEW DIRECTION

It was the third day of the off-site, and the energy in the room was noticeably different from the start. Everyone had arrived early, eager to get to work, coffee cups in hand and doughnuts passed around. There was a sense of accomplishment in the air as the team settled into their seats, ready for what they all hoped would be the day they solidified Clearview's new direction.

TJ Strong stood at the front of the room, pausing to take in the sight of his department heads chatting casually, laughing, and reflecting on the past few days. It was a stark contrast to the strained silence that had marked their first meeting. The team had come a long way in just two days, and TJ couldn't help but feel proud.

"Alright, everyone," TJ said, bringing the room to order. "Before we dive in today, let's quickly review what we've accomplished so far."

The team nodded as Rick, the interim Planning director, raised his hand. "I've been thinking a lot about the mission statement we developed last week, and I think we're missing something. It brought me back to what Chief Ashton said about the coast guard and their motto. What do you all think about creating an internal message to go along with the mission statement, some sort of rallying cry that the employees can really get behind?"

The room buzzed with murmurs of agreement. Jamie was the first to speak. "I love that idea, Rick. We need something short, powerful, and memorable—something that gets the team excited about where we're going."

Darnell nodded in agreement. "Yeah, something that'll remind us why we're here and what we're working toward—a rallying cry that keeps everyone focused on solutions."

Just as the discussion was gaining momentum, TJ glanced at his phone and frowned slightly. He had a call scheduled with councilwoman Kim Bolder, and while it wasn't urgent, it was something that had been lingering on his mind. He knew it could wait until the break, but an idea struck him—this might be a good opportunity to see how the team handled things on their own. They were coming together, and giving them a little space to collaborate without him might be the perfect test of how far they'd come.

"Hey, I hate to step out right when we're getting into this," TJ said, standing up, "but I need to make a quick call to Councilwoman Bolder. I'll leave you all to brainstorm without me for a few minutes."

Jamie raised an eyebrow. "You sure? We could wait."

TJ shrugged, smiling. "Yeah, but I think you've got this. I'll be back soon."

Jamie replied with a bit of playful sarcasm, "We will handle it, but I do seem to remember someone saying no phones will be answered at the off-site"

As TJ stepped out of the room, he couldn't help but chuckle to himself. "Let's see how far they've come," he muttered under his breath as he dialed Kim's number.

Kim Bolder had been on the city council for two years now. A stay-at-home mom before reentering the workforce, she was known for her advocacy of parks programs, the library, and supporting local businesses. But she was also frustrated—frustrated with the inefficiency of the city's operations and the often-rude treatment that residents faced from city employees. She had become fed up with the difficulty of working with Clearview and knew that many people had stopped taking jobs within city limits altogether. Despite this, Kim had a soft spot for the employees and was hesitant to push for big changes, hoping that everyone could succeed under the right leadership.

"Hi, Kim. It's TJ," he greeted her warmly as she picked up.

"TJ, thanks for calling," Kim said, though her tone hinted at frustration. "I've been meaning to talk to you about something."

"What's going on?" TJ asked, already bracing himself for what was likely another complaint about customer service.

"A friend of mine called the city yesterday to pay her utility bill, and she had a really unpleasant experience. She said the clerk was rude and then told her that the city doesn't take payments over the phone. My friend was really upset, and honestly, so am I."

The energy sparked by the off-site began to leave TJ's body. This wasn't the first time he'd heard this kind of complaint. "I understand, Kim. I'm really sorry your friend had that experience. I'll call her directly to resolve the issue. As for the phone payment policy, I'll take a look at it and see if there's something we can change to make things smoother. I do know that there are some issues with our software that need to be resolved."

"I appreciate that, TJ," Kim replied, her voice softening. "I just want to see our city operating efficiently, you know? People shouldn't feel like they're being mistreated."

"I completely agree," TJ said. "We're actually working on some changes as we speak. I'll make sure this issue gets addressed."

After a few more minutes of calming Kim down and

promising to follow up, TJ hung up and immediately called the complainant. He explained the city's policy on phone payments but listened to her frustrations and assured her that they would find a better solution moving forward. By the time the call ended, the situation was resolved, and TJ felt confident that both Kim and her friend were satisfied.

When TJ returned to the meeting room, he was greeted by the sound of laughter. The team was fully engaged, tossing around ideas and clearly having a good time. Kevin was teasing Jamie about one of her suggestions, and she was playfully defending herself.

"Well, looks like the party's going just fine without me," TJ said, the smile returning to his face as he walked in.

"We've got something for you!" Darnell announced, grinning. "We've been working on a rallying cry, and we think we've got it."

TJ raised an eyebrow, curious. "Let's hear it."

"Try not to make TJ mad," Walter said, barely able to keep from laughing out loud.

TJ looked at the team with a side-eye. "Well, I guess that's something . . ." Everyone laughed.

"Well," Jamie said with a smile. "If you are not going to let that one go, how about 'Improving Clearview, one solution at a time.'"

TJ paused for a moment, letting the words sink in. It was simple, but it captured the essence of what they were trying to achieve. "I love it," he said finally. "It's exactly what we need. It's focused on solutions and progress, which is the direction we're heading."

The team nodded in agreement, clearly pleased with their work.

After a quick morning break, TJ gathered everyone back together to start the day's main task—laying out the steps needed to change the city's culture. They had established core values yesterday. Now it was time to figure out the rest of the framework for a solution-focused culture.

TJ stood at the front of the room and wrote on the board: **Step 1: Evaluate the Organization.**

"This is what I have been doing for the last several months and you have been doing for the last week. If you remember, when I tasked you with surveying your team, we discussed not solving anything at the moment and that we were collecting data. The data you collected, combined with the public satisfaction survey, the employee satisfaction survey, and my ride-alongs, will give us the information necessary to understand the current condition and what we need to focus on. While we will have to keep revisiting this, I believe we have enough information at this time to move past this step."

Looking around, TJ saw everyone nodding.

Confident that there were no questions, TJ wrote on the board: **Step 2: Establish a Mission and Core Values.**

"We have also already done this part," TJ said, gesturing to the core values they created the day before and the mission statement from the previous week. "But now we need to talk about how to make those values effective."

Rick raised his hand. "I think the next step is explaining how the core values connect to the mission and how they do their job. It's one thing to have values, but people need to understand how those values and their job here at the city fit into what we're trying to accomplish."

TJ nodded, writing: **Step 3: Explain – Explain How the Core Values Connect to the Mission and the Work.**

The team spent the next half hour discussing how they could communicate the core values to their staff, ensuring that everyone understood the connection between the values and the city's broader mission. Ideas flowed freely, with everyone participating in the conversation, offering stories and insights that helped bring the values to life.

Eventually, Jamie stood up and wrote on the board: **Step 4: Engage – Engage the Team in Developing a Strategy.**

"This is where we talk about getting the subject matter experts involved," she said. "The people who are closest to the problems need to be the ones working on the solutions."

TJ stepped in. "Exactly. And there's a big difference between buy-in and ownership. If we sell an idea to the team, they might go along with it, but they won't be as invested. But if they have ownership in the idea, they will be much more committed to making it work."

The team nodded, clearly understanding the distinction. They continued to build on the idea of engaging the staff, sharing examples from research they had done earlier in the week. The consensus was clear: employees needed to feel empowered to take ownership of the solutions rather than just following orders.

By the time they had finished discussing engagement, it was nearly lunchtime. Rather than break the momentum, the team decided to order in and keep working through lunch. As they waited for their food, the conversation became more lighthearted, with team members cracking jokes and teasing each other. It was clear that the group had become more than just colleagues—they were becoming a true team.

As lunch arrived, Frank leaned back in his chair and smiled. "I've got to say, I've really enjoyed this process. I wasn't sure about it at first, but it's been great to see how we're all coming together."

Walter nodded in agreement. "Yeah, it feels like we're finally getting on the same page. We're not just talking about change—we're making it happen."

After lunch, the team reconvened, and TJ moved on to the next step. "So, we've talked about establishing core values, explaining them, and engaging the team. The next logical step is to empower the team to solve problems using the core values and mission as a guide."

Jamie stood up and walked to the board, writing: **Step 5: Empower – Give Employees the Authority to Make Decisions.**

"We need to let the team solve problems at the lowest competent level," Jamie said. "They shouldn't have to wait for approval on every little thing. If they know what needs to be done, we should trust them to do it."

The team loved the idea, and they began discussing examples from their earlier surveys and ride-alongs, pointing out how this approach would have made certain situations easier to resolve. They talked about how empowering employees would lead to faster decisions and better service for the public.

TJ stood at the front of the room and said, "I guess that's it —five steps to a solution-focused culture."

"I think something is missing," Carrie said. She then walked over to the board and wrote the final step: **Step 6: Experience Success.**

"I really believe if we follow the steps, we will experience success," she said.

"I think you are right. This is where we see the results," TJ said. "If we follow these steps—establish core values, explain them, engage the team, empower them—we'll experience success. Success will come naturally because the foundation is solid. Not to mention, success is contagious. Once it starts, it spreads and breeds more success."

The team all took pictures of the 6 Es of a solution-focused culture on the board, feeling satisfied with their accomplishments. The atmosphere in the room was one of fulfillment and excitement for what lay ahead.

As the day came to a close, the team began planning an all-staff training day, where they could bring everyone together to roll out the new plan for Clearview's culture. There would be a lunch, and TJ would present the new framework, ensuring that every employee understood the direction the city was heading.

As the team left the conference room, they felt a sense of pride and accomplishment. They had laid the foundation for a solution-focused culture, and now it was time to bring it to life. TJ watched them go, knowing that this was just the beginning—but it was a very promising start.

CHAPTER 11
GETTING THE TEAM ONBOARD

The morning of the all-staff meeting had arrived. The day was set to be a mix of training, camaraderie, and a hopeful new start for the city employees of Clearview. TJ pulled into the park just as the sun was beginning to rise over the tree line. "This is going to be a great day," he thought as he opened the car door and felt a crisp breeze. He immediately spotted Darnell, who was already unloading games and boxes of supplies. On the other side of the event area, Jamie was helping set up tables near the pavilion.

"Morning, Boss!" Darnell called out with his usual enthusiasm, waving as TJ stepped out of his car. "I think we are going to have some fun today! I know my team is really looking forward to some downtime."

"Morning," TJ replied with a grin, walking over to give them a hand. "Agreed! Looks like everything is in order."

Jamie smiled, adjusting a stack of paper plates on one of the tables. "I agree. I really think this will be a great day. My team is looking forward to spending some time with their friends from other departments. It's the first time the city has done something like this in a long time."

TJ glanced around the park, noticing that some employees were starting to show up early while the park was coming alive in the morning sun. The last few weeks had been a whirlwind for him, but he felt a real sense of accomplishment this morning.

After the off-site, the leadership group continued to grow as a team. They were working together more effectively, even as the city itself wrestled with its longstanding regulatory identity. They were far from where they needed to be, but TJ had seen real progress in how the executive team interacted. Instead of letting problems simmer or ignoring them, they had started calling emergency strategy meetings, collaborating to find solutions in ways they hadn't before. Issues that would have once festered or been met with finger-pointing were now being addressed head-on.

But today was about the staff, and it would be critical to get everyone on board. The leadership team was excited about grilling burgers and spending time with the staff in a relaxed setting. It would be a good opportunity to talk openly about the new mission statement, core values, and strategy to move the city forward.

"So," Darnell said, snapping TJ out of his thoughts, "you ready for today, Boss?"

"Yeah, let's get this show on the road," TJ said, rubbing his hands together, excitement buzzing in his veins.

As they set up the last of the details—checking the microphones, arranging chairs, setting out games, and preparing food—TJ, Darnell, and Jamie talked about how much they hoped the day would bring everyone together. "I think everyone's starting to feel the changes," Jamie said thoughtfully. "I hear people talking about it in the halls. Some are skeptical, of course, but there's definitely more excitement than I expected."

Darnell agreed, flipping a couple of bean bags at the cornhole boards he had just set up. "Yeah, I've heard some of the same. We've still got a long way to go, but if we can get people feeling like they're part of the solution instead of just following orders, I think we'll be on the right track."

TJ smiled at the thought. The off-site had been the start of something important, but this event would, or he thought could, be the start of real positive change. It was the next big step in transforming Clearview's culture. He just hoped the employees would be as receptive as the leadership team had been.

A couple of hours later, the park was buzzing with activity. Employees were milling about, grabbing coffee and doughnuts, chatting with each other as they waited for the day to begin. A large banner reading "A Solution-Focused Culture" stretched across the stage.

As the chairs filled up, Mayor Whitmore, a friendly man with silver hair and a big presence, took the stage first to address the staff. He cleared his throat, gripping the microphone a little too tightly.

"Good morning, everyone," Mayor Whitmore said with a warm smile. His voice boomed through the speakers. "I want to start by thanking you for coming out today. I just want to take a moment to express how much I appreciate the hard work each and every one of you do for this city. We are a growing comm-unity, and with growth comes challenges. I know we have the right people in place to meet those challenges head-on. We've got a fantastic leadership team here, and under TJ's guidance, we're moving in the right direction. I won't take up any more time; let's make the most of today and have some fun along the way! Thank you!"

The crowd offered polite applause as Mayor Whitmore stepped down. TJ took a breath and turned on his lapel microphone as he walked up to the front of the crowd. There was a swell of anticipation as he looked out over the gathered staff. This was his chance to connect with them directly and share the vision for Clearview's future.

"Good morning, everyone," TJ greeted the crowd. "I'm glad to see so many of you here today. Over the last few weeks, I've had the privilege of getting to know many of you better, and I can't tell you how excited I am about where we're headed. A few weeks ago, the leadership team and I started the process of developing a strategy for the future of Clearview. We spent a lot of time reflecting on the challenges we face, but more importantly, we focused on two things: creating an environment where you enjoy coming to work and developing a new system of doing business."

TJ glanced over at the leadership team, who were all seated in front of the crowd, giving them a slight nod before continuing. "What came out of that meeting is something we're calling a *solution-focused culture*. It's not just about solving problems as they come up—it's about changing how we approach everything we do. It's about empowering every single person in this organization to make decisions, to be part of the solution, not just follow orders or pass problems up the chain."

TJ clicked a button on the small remote he held, and the

large screen behind him displayed the new mission statement the city council had developed: "To make Clearview the most desirable city to live, work, and play."

"This is our new mission statement," TJ explained. "It's simple but powerful. And it's something we can all contribute to, no matter what department you're in. Whether you're at Public Works, the Police Department, Parks and Rec, or the Finance Office, every one of us has a role in making Clearview the best it can be."

TJ shifted gears. "But a mission statement is just the beginning, so we could not stop there. We also developed what we're calling the *6 Es*—a framework for how we're going to get there. I will walk you through those now, but I want you all to think about how each of these steps applies to the work you do every day."

He turned to the board behind him, where the 6 Es were written in bold:

1. **Evaluate the Current Condition**
2. **Establish Core Values**
3. **Explain How the Core Values Connect to Our Mission**
4. **Engage the Team in Developing a Strategy**
5. **Empower Employees to Make Decisions**
6. **Experience Success**

"Over the last few months, the department heads and I have been meeting with many of you and discussing what can be improved within the departments. We have talked about policies, systems, and a lack of resources that make your jobs difficult. During this time, we worked through the first step of the process, which was evaluating the current condition of operations."

TJ could tell that many of the employees were recognizing

for the first time that all of the meetings and each ride-along were to gain an understanding of their needs.

Appreciating that the team was beginning to understand the process, TJ continued, "Over the last few weeks, your department heads have been sharing with you the core values recently developed by the leadership team and adopted by the city council." He pointed to the second E: Establish Core Values. "These values—transparency, respect, accountability, innovation, teamwork, and selflessness—are what will guide everything we do moving forward. You can see that these values spell out TRAITS. These values represent the *traits* we will look for in all Clearview employees," TJ said, looking at the crowd as most nodded. "The first two steps are done. Now, it's time to work through the rest of these."

The crowd appeared engaged, maintaining eye contact and nodding as TJ spoke. He felt the momentum building.

"I want to do something a little different now," TJ said. "I'm going to call on a few of you to talk about how your job connects to one of these core values. Does anyone feel like sharing today?" TJ waited nervously for someone to step forward.

With some relief, TJ noticed Brandon Simmons, the officer he had spent a shift with, standing to speak. "Let's start with Officer Simmons."

Brandon stood up eagerly. He had been one of the more skeptical employees when TJ joined him on a ride-along shortly after starting at the city, but something had shifted in him over the last few weeks.

"I think about accountability a lot," Brandon said, his voice confident. "As a police officer, it's important that I hold myself to a high standard. If I'm not accountable for my actions, how can I expect the community to trust me? It's the same for all of us. If we hold ourselves accountable, the public will start to see that we're serious about making Clearview better."

GETTING THE TEAM ONBOARD

The crowd erupted with applause, and TJ beamed. Brandon had hit the nail on the head.

As the conversation continued, TJ moved through the rest of the 6 Es, calling on different employees to discuss how each step in the process would impact their jobs. When they reached empowerment, both Mary from engineering and Teri from parks spoke up.

"I'm really excited about this idea of empowerment," Mary said. "There have been so many times when I've known exactly how to solve a problem, but I had to wait for approval from three or four people before I could do anything about it. Now, with this new approach, I feel like I'll actually be able to help people in real time."

Teri nodded in agreement. "Same here. In parks, we deal with so many small issues—people reserving fields, dealing with damaged equipment—things that we could handle quickly if we were given more authority. I'm excited to see how this changes the way we work."

Somewhat surprisingly for TJ, Carol, a clerk in the utilities division, who was usually more reserved, chimed in. "On the way in this morning, I noticed the signup sheets for the process improvement teams. I am thinking about signing up. I think we have a lot of opportunities to streamline things, especially with billing. If we can figure out a way to improve our internal processes, we can give better service to our customers."

The energy in the room was palpable. TJ could see the excitement growing, and as he wrapped up his presentation, he knew they were on the right track.

When they broke for lunch, the leadership team took to the grills, flipping burgers and chatting with employees as they came through the line. The sun was high in the sky now, casting a warm glow over the park. The smell of burgers and hot dogs filled the air, and the sound of laughter and conversation buzzed around them.

As TJ stood behind the grill, spatula in hand, he couldn't help but feel an overwhelming sense of optimism. It wasn't just the success of the day—it was the sense that the entire team was starting to believe in the vision they had worked so hard to create.

The police chief walked over, grabbing a plate. "I've got to say, TJ," he said, taking a bite of his burger, "I wasn't sure about all this at first. But over the last few days, I've really enjoyed the process. I think we're onto something."

Walter nodded as he joined them. "Same here. It feels like we're finally working together instead of against each other. I'm glad to see the staff is on board too."

The rest of the day flew by, filled with games, discussions, and casual conversations about the future. TJ watched as employees from different departments mingled, sharing ideas and stories. The sense of division that had once hung over the city was starting to fade, replaced by a feeling of unity and purpose.

At one point, TJ and Carrie joined in a game of cornhole playing for opposite teams. Much of the finance staff looked on, cheering Carrie on as she beat TJ handily.

As the sun began to set, TJ took a moment to reflect. The journey wasn't over, and there was still plenty of work to be done. But for the first time since he had arrived in Clearview, TJ felt like they were on the right path. The solution-focused culture they had talked about so much was no longer just an idea—it was becoming a reality.

And for the first time in a long time, TJ was genuinely optimistic about the future.

CHAPTER 12
THIS MIGHT WORK

Just before dawn, TJ sat at the kitchen table sipping his coffee. The sun had yet to rise, and the house was quiet except for the gentle clatter of dishes as his wife, Dawn, moved about preparing breakfast. The success of the recent all-staff day lingered in his thoughts. The day had gone better than expected, with employees showing genuine interest in the new solution-focused culture. But now, it was time to get back to the reality of work. The excitement of that day had to be translated into everyday practices, and he knew that wouldn't be easy.

Dawn slid a plate of scrambled eggs, fresh from their backyard chicken coop, in front of him and sat down. A faint crease appeared on her forehead, hinting at her concern. "So, how do you think today's going to go?" she asked, breaking into her thoughts.

TJ took a deep breath. "I think it'll be fine. The team has really bought into the whole solution-focused thing. I've seen the change starting already. We've had a few strategy meetings since the off-site, and people have really been stepping up."

Dawn's eyes met his as she questioned, "You're not worried about them losing momentum? Sometimes it's easy to be excited about something new in the moment, but it can be hard to keep that energy going once the day-to-day stuff hits."

TJ smiled, reaching for her hand. "I'm confident. This isn't just a one-time thing. We've got a framework now, a real process. The culture is starting to shift, and I think the team is ready to put it to work." He leaned back, finishing his coffee. "Besides, we've all committed to this. I think they'll stay the course."

Dawn smiled, though a trace of concern remained. "Well, I hope you're right. You've worked so hard to get to this point. Just remember, sometimes change takes time."

TJ nodded. He was ready, he felt it in his gut. He kissed her on the cheek, grabbed his keys, and headed out the door, ready to face whatever challenges the day brought. "Love you, baby. See ya soon."

At the office, TJ's first stop was Jamie's desk. She was already there, typing furiously at her computer, as organized and efficient as ever. TJ tapped lightly on the edge of her cubicle to get her attention.

"Morning, Jamie. How're we looking after the all-staff day?"

Jamie turned and smiled. "Morning, Boss! I think it went really well. I've been hearing a lot of good feedback. People are talking about the 6 Es and connecting them to their work. It's actually kind of amazing to see how quickly the idea caught on."

"Great to hear," TJ replied, genuinely pleased. "We've got some big meetings today though. Space Experts is coming in for their development review. I expect that to be . . . interesting."

Jamie raised an eyebrow. "Yeah, I've seen that on your

calendar. Good luck with that one. It's not looking good for them with the location they've picked."

Just then, TJ's executive assistant walked by with her usual brisk pace. She gave him a look that only a well-seasoned assistant could, the kind that said, "I know something's up."

"Morning, Christine," TJ called. "Everything OK?"

Christine stopped, hands full of folders, and gave a small, strained smile. "Good morning, TJ. Yes, mostly. I put Space Experts on your schedule today. I just wanted to give you a heads-up. Rick came by and said they wanted to meet with you. It looks like the location they're proposing is going to be a problem. Zoning issues, stormwater drainage . . . you name it. You've got until 4:00 p.m. to come up with a plan."

TJ sighed inwardly. "Great. Anything else I should know about?"

Christine patted him on the arm and grinned. "I'm sure you'll figure it out. But, yes, Councilman Evans is here to see you. He's waiting in your office." She gave him a knowing look. "Act like you have some sense, Boss."

TJ felt a wave of weariness. Of course, Sam Evans would show up unannounced. He was a constant figure in Clearview's political life, often with concerns or complaints from his network of friends and associates. TJ nodded to Christine. "Don't I always act like I have some sense? Send him in."

As TJ settled into his office, Mr. Evans came in, not bothering to sit down right away. He was clearly frustrated, and TJ could already guess where this conversation was headed.

"TJ," he started, "I need your help. A good friend of mine is trying to open a restaurant in one of those old warehouses on the east side of town, but the city's telling him no. Now, I don't understand why. If it used to be a manufacturing plant, why can't he just turn it into a restaurant?"

TJ took a deep breath and motioned for Evans to sit. "Councilman Evans, I hear you. But it's not as simple as that. The zoning for that area hasn't been updated in years, and converting a manufacturing space into a restaurant isn't a straight shot. There are issues with parking, safety regulations, and many other factors we have to consider."

Evans frowned, crossing his arms. "But this city needs more businesses like his. You and I both know that. We're trying to grow, right? So why aren't we making it easier for people to open businesses?"

TJ leaned forward, meeting the councilman's gaze. "You're right that we need more businesses, but we also have to make sure we're doing it the right way. I'm not saying no to your friend. I'm saying we need to find a way to do it that works for everyone."

Mr. Evans seemed to soften a little, but he still wasn't happy. "I don't know, TJ. He's frustrated. I just need you to figure something out."

TJ nodded. "I'll work on it, Sam. I can't guarantee anything right now, but I'll take a look at the situation and see what we can do."

After a few more minutes of conversation, he left, still grumbling but at least somewhat appeased. TJ leaned back in his chair, running his hands through his hair. It wasn't even noon yet, and the day was already shaping up to be a mess.

He pressed the intercom to Christine. "Hey, Christine? Could you come in for a minute?"

Christine stuck her head in the door a moment later, a smirk on her face. "Need me to book you a flight out of town with all the chaos going on today? I hear Europe is good this time of year."

TJ laughed, shaking his head. "As fun as that sounds, no. Today's a day for solutions. I need you to set up an emergency meeting with the team. I want the executive leadership team, the city engineer, the planner, the building official, and the fire marshal. We need to figure out how we will fix these projects."

Christine nodded, her smirk widening. "OK, your choice. I'll get everyone in the conference room in thirty. Don't say I didn't try . . ."

TJ, laughing, said, "I always appreciate your willingness to book me a flight out of the country, but instead, can you see if Rick has a minute for me to stop by before the meeting?"

"Sure, I'll have him come by in fifteen minutes," she said.

On his way to the meeting, TJ stopped by and talked with Rick about his work over the last few months as the interim director. The two talked about the future of the city and what was needed for the department. The conversation resulted in TJ asking Rick if he would consider taking the role of director permanently. Rick graciously accepted.

By the time TJ walked into the conference room, the air was buzzing with tension. The usual leadership crew was seated, along with Mary, the city engineer; Rick, the recently promoted planning director; and Kevin, the fire marshal. Everyone looked up as TJ entered and wrote two words at the top of the whiteboard: *Solution-Focused.*

Beneath that, TJ drew three columns, labeling them with the three main projects causing trouble: Space Experts, the shopping center from the month before, and the restaurant that Councilman Evans had just told him about.

"Alright," TJ said, turning to face the group. "It's time to put our plan to work. None of these projects can go where the owners want them, but we all want them here. So how are we going to solve this?"

Immediately, the room came alive with ideas. Rick started discussing zoning changes while Mary dove into the specifics of the stormwater issues with the Space Experts site. Kevin chimed in with safety concerns for the restaurant, but he also mentioned knowing the warehouse owner and offered to reach out to help facilitate discussions.

"We could work with the owner of the land near the shopping center," Darnell said, leaning forward. "If they're flexible, we might be able to shift the development just enough to make it work."

"I think we can suggest a new layout for Space Experts," Mary added, her eyes lighting up. "If we reconfigure the stormwater plan, it might solve the issue. I'll make some calls."

The meeting carried on for hours, with everyone fully engaged. By the time the afternoon rolled around, they had solutions in place for all three projects. Mary's adjustments to the Space Experts site plan made the development feasible, and Kevin's contact with the warehouse owner meant the restaurant could work with the city on a safe conversion. Even the shopping center, which had been in limbo for a month, had a path forward.

As the clock neared 7:00 p.m., the room was still buzzing. Phones rang as developers and landowners were called, meetings were rearranged, and plans were revised. By the time everyone finally packed up to leave, the projects were on the path to success.

As the last few people filtered out, Walter, the Public Works director, stayed behind. He walked over to the whiteboard and circled the words *Solution-Focused* with a grin.

"I think you did it, Boss," Walter said, giving TJ a pat on the back.

TJ looked at the board, feeling a deep sense of satisfaction. "No, Walter," he said, smiling, "*we* did it."

Just then, Christine popped her head through the doorway. "Hey, TJ, do you want me to go ahead and order that new chair?"

TJ chuckled, glancing around the room. "You know, Christine, I think this place is finally starting to fit right. I think I'll go just with it."

As they left the office, TJ couldn't help but feel that despite the chaos, the team was truly beginning to embody the solution-focused culture they had worked so hard to create. For the first time, they weren't just talking about change—they were living it.

CHAPTER 13
SUCCESS!

A year had passed since that chaotic day in the conference room, where the team had worked relentlessly to find solutions for the projects that had once seemed impossible. TJ Strong pushed open the heavy glass door of Mikey's, the familiar smell of grilled steaks and freshly baked rolls greeting him as he stepped inside. It was a smell that, for TJ, now carried the sweet scent of accomplishment. He was arriving late after attending the ribbon cutting for Space Experts' new manufacturing facility, a project that had become the crowning achievement of his first year as Clearview's city manager.

The Space Experts facility was more than just another building in the city. It was a symbol of the transformation that had taken place in Clearview, both within the city government and in the community. The state-of-the-art facility sprawled across a previously underutilized part of town, offering two hundred new jobs—many of them paying well above the median income. Some of the positions were even double the median, something Clearview desperately needed. It hadn't been an easy journey to get there, but as TJ listened to the company's CEO share their reasons for choosing

Clearview at the ribbon cutting earlier that day, a deep sense of pride had welled up in him.

"We had other options, other cities that would have welcomed us with open arms," the CEO had said from the podium. "But Clearview was the one place where we didn't just hear 'no' when we ran into challenges. Instead, we were met with a team that worked with us to solve problems. The staff here found creative solutions to help us make this facility a reality, and that's why we're here today."

Councilman Cho had stood proudly by the CEO's side, beaming as the crowd applauded. TJ had clapped along with them, but his mind had been elsewhere. He had been thinking about the journey the city had taken to get here, about how far they'd come in just a year. He could still remember the tense meetings, the long nights, and the tough decisions, but now, standing at that ribbon cutting, all of it seemed worth it.

As TJ approached the table where Dawn and the kids were already seated, his wife looked up and smiled, that warm, knowing smile she always gave him when he walked in after a long day. The kids were chatting excitedly about their day. TJ gave Dawn a kiss before he sat down beside her.

"Big day, huh?" she asked, her eyes twinkling as she reached for his hand under the table.

TJ nodded, exhaling slowly. "Yeah, you could say that. I still can't believe we pulled it off."

Dawn grinned. "Of course you did. You've been working so hard. Look at everything that's changed. Oh, by the way, I ran into Karen earlier today. She was telling me that their son just got hired at Thread Max, that new national clothing store that opened in the shopping center."

TJ raised an eyebrow, intrigued. "Really? That's great."

"Yeah," Dawn continued. "She said they're thrilled. Apparently, he's been looking for something steady, and this was exactly what he needed."

TJ smiled as he took it all in. The shopping center had been one of the more frustrating projects early on. There had been so many hurdles, many times it looked like the development would fall through. But the team had stayed focused, finding solutions that allowed the space to be remodeled and transformed into something new. The national clothing store was just one of the tenants that had moved in, bringing jobs and revitalizing an area that had been a bit of a dead zone for years.

As TJ sat with his family, his mind wandered again, reflecting on all the progress they had made. It wasn't just the big projects like Space Experts and the shopping center that had truly shifted; it was the culture within the city government. The solution-focused approach they had worked so hard to implement was no longer just an idea—they were living it.

The city staff had embraced the 6 Es, and the impact was visible. Employees solved problems at the lowest level and were empowered to make decisions without waiting for approval from higher-ups. Departments collaborated more than ever before, and the finger-pointing and blame-shifting that had once been so common had been replaced with a sense of teamwork and shared purpose. The city wasn't perfect—there were still challenges to overcome—but for the first time in years, it felt like everyone was rowing in the same direction.

He glanced around Mikey's, smiling at the bustling restaurant and the familiar faces of the staff, who seemed to enjoy their work as much as ever. Mikey had always told him that the secret to his restaurant's success was the culture he had built, one where the employees felt like they were part of something bigger. It was a lesson TJ had taken to heart, and now, sitting in the same restaurant a year later, he could see that lesson paying off.

Suddenly, he felt a tap on his shoulder. He turned to see

Carol from the utility department standing there, grinning from ear to ear.

"TJ! I just wanted to say hi," Carol said, bouncing slightly on her heels excitedly.

"Hey, Carol! How are you?" TJ replied, genuinely happy to see her.

"Oh, I'm great! I just had to tell you—I love the new software we've been using. It's made everything so much easier. We can finally process things faster, and customers are actually thanking us now!" She laughed. "I never thought I'd hear that!"

TJ chuckled, pleased to hear her enthusiasm. The new software had been one of those projects that had dragged on for months, with delays and budget issues nearly derailing it several times. But now, hearing Carol's excitement, TJ knew it had been worth every bit of effort.

They chatted for a few more minutes, Carol sharing updates about the department before she excused herself and returned to her table. TJ watched her go, smiling to himself. Moments like that, small but significant, made him realize just how much had changed.

As he turned back to his meal, he noticed that Dawn had been watching him, her eyes sparkling with amusement.

"You're reminiscing again, aren't you?" she teased, nudging him gently.

"Maybe a little," TJ admitted with a laugh. "It's just crazy to think about where we were a year ago and where we are now. We've come so far, and sometimes it feels like it happened overnight."

Dawn squeezed his hand. "You've done an amazing job, TJ. You should be proud."

"I am," he said quietly, smiling at her. "But it wasn't just me. The team stepped up. Everyone played a part in getting us here."

Just then, Mikey himself walked over to their table, a wide

grin on his face. "TJ! Good to see you, my friend," Mikey said, shaking his hand warmly. "How's everything going?"

"Couldn't be better, Mikey. How about you? Still claiming to have the best job in town?" TJ asked with a playful grin.

Mikey laughed, clapping TJ on the back. "Oh, you know it! I get to feed people great food every day and make them happy. Can't beat that."

TJ smirked, leaning back in his chair. "I don't know, Mikey. After the year I've had, I think I might have you beat. I get to help build a city."

Mikey raised an eyebrow, laughing heartily. "Well, looks like I've got some competition then."

As Mikey wandered off to greet more customers, TJ took a deep breath, the warm atmosphere of the restaurant settling around him. For the first time in a long time, he felt a deep sense of peace. Clearview was thriving, not just because of the new developments or the jobs created, but because the city's culture had transformed. They had built something sustainable, something that would carry them forward for years to come.

As TJ sat there, surrounded by his family, friends, and a community he had helped strengthen, he bowed his head to bless the food and thank God for the blessings in his life, for he knew without a doubt that he truly had the best job in the world.

AFTERWARD

Thank you for accompanying us on the journey through Clearview's transformation. We hope you found insights and inspiration along the way. As we close, we trust that the experiences shared here have sparked ideas for your own path toward meaningful change.

As you move into the next sections, we will walk you through a detailed, step-by-step guide to implementing transformative changes like those that reshaped Clearview. The following six practical steps are designed to provide actionable tools and strategies to help you build a workplace culture that not only supports but also encourages leadership, innovation, and collaboration at all levels. Whether you're aiming to enhance team dynamics, improve decision-making processes, or create an environment where creativity thrives, this guide offers a comprehensive roadmap.

Each step is crafted to empower you with techniques to address common workplace challenges, align your team's values with organizational goals, and cultivate a supportive environment where every member can excel. By the end of this journey, you will have the resources and insights

AFTERWARD

necessary to create a culture that values solution-focused approaches and continuous improvement.

If you're looking for additional tools, resources, or personalized guidance, visit our online resource hub at http://www.solution-focusedculture.com, where you'll find templates, case studies, and expert advice tailored to fostering a thriving workplace culture.

Enjoy the rest of the book, and best of luck on your journey toward building a solution-focused culture that inspires and drives success in your organization.

STEP 1: EVALUATE

Every organization has a culture, good or bad, whether intentional or accidental. In a solution-focused culture, we develop an intentional system of innovation by reinforcing the values and behaviors that drive success. *Organizational culture* refers to a system of shared assumptions, values, and beliefs that show people what is appropriate and inappropriate behavior (Chatman and Eunyoung 2003; Kerr and Slocum 2005).

Before any organization can begin the journey toward a solution-focused culture, the leadership must first gain a deep understanding of the current needs of its stakeholders. For the purpose of this section, stakeholders will include the governing board, executive leadership, team members, customers, citizens, and property owners. We believe it is important to engage all stakeholder groups in this initial process because each group brings their unique perspectives, challenges, and goals to the table. Understanding how they fit together is essential for any cultural transformation. This section outlines a comprehensive approach to assessing the current condition of the organization through targeted surveys and direct engagement. Collecting high-quality information at this point is critical, as it provides the solid foundation necessary to foster a solution-oriented mindset.

In the story, TJ and Jamie discuss several different approaches to gathering information, including the utilization of electronic surveys. TJ also calls for the leadership team to conduct informal "rounding" style inquiries to gain firsthand insight into the overall work environment, including the quantity *and* quality of resources available to staff and convoluted policies that prevent efficient progress. These approaches enabled them to learn more about the condition of the organization by seeing it through the eyes of the staff.

A successful transformation starts with understanding the current condition of the organization. From leadership expectations and employee mindset to customer experience, both internal and external factors must be considered. The goal is to ensure that the services provided meet the needs of the community in a way that is efficient, effective, and satisfying. Culture is developed and cultivated at the top of the organization; therefore, implementing any real culture change must start at the top as well. For this reason, we begin with the board of directors and executive leadership team.

Discover

In local government, like many other organizations, our governing body is a board of directors. The board, whether it be a council or commission, sets the direction for the organization, the mission, and the guidelines for accomplishing this mission. To initiate change, the leadership team must first discover the priorities and desires of the board. To successfully implement organizational change, the governing board must recognize the need and support the process. The strategic planning process is a common tool used to bring a board together and determine their priorities. This process involves a variety of stakeholders, most importantly board members and the senior leadership team, but should also engage staff members and be open for public comment. Crafting a strategic plan involves defining the organization's mission, vision, and values through a SWOT analysis that identifies internal and external strengths, weaknesses, opportunities, and threats. Once completed, you must set targeted and measurable goals and objectives. Strategies are then developed to achieve these objectives, followed by detailed action plans that outline specific steps, responsibilities, and timelines.

Align

Understanding the perspectives and goals of the executive leadership team is the next piece of the assessment process. Even though the leadership team often envisions the organization's future, it's vital that their objectives remain aligned with the core mission and the on-the-ground realities.

To do this, we start with the senior leadership team. They must engage in an open and honest discussion as a team about their understanding of the organization's mission and how they see their roles in achieving it. Questions to consider include the following:

- Why does this organization exist? What is our why?
- What do we do best as an organization?
- What does success look like?
- How do you see the mission play out in our day-to-day?
- What do you see as the biggest obstacles facing our organization today?
- Where do you see opportunities for our team to improve the customer experience?
- What happens if we fail in the mission?

STEP 1: EVALUATE

Often, while answering the questions above, the team will learn that there is a lack of alignment between members of the team concerning the organization's true mission. When this happens, the team must go back through this process again and again until they gain alignment in this area. If the leadership team is clear, the rest of the organization will follow. If not, it will be impossible to create a solution-focused culture. When leadership participates openly and honestly in these types of discussions, only then can they discern the true state of the organization.

Learn

With the leadership team now on the same page and focused on achieving the overall mission, they can begin to learn about the organization's needs. Because external feedback often takes longer to gather, we suggest that you begin by collecting detailed feedback directly from customers about their interactions with the organization. One effective way to collect this feedback is through surveys.

Electronic surveys can be sent to customers immediately after a service interaction, such as after applying for a permit or after the completion of a program like youth soccer. These surveys are often low cost, require a smaller time commitment, and offer an increased feeling of anonymity. They frequently utilize mobile-friendly technology so a customer can complete them from their smartphone by utilizing a QR code or shortened URL. We encourage you to use both open-ended and closed-ended questions, such as the following:

- How would you rate your overall satisfaction?
- Was the time it took to resolve your request satisfactory?
- Did you find the process to be easy?
- Did you find the staff to be helpful?
- What would have improved your experience?

STEP 1: EVALUATE

- Would you like to provide any additional suggestions that would have improved your customer experience?

By including both open-ended and closed-ended questions, organizations will capture both quantitative and qualitative data.

Some customers may not feel comfortable with electronic surveys, or they may just prefer a more personal approach. In this case, over-the-phone surveys can be an effective tool. While this type of survey provides a personal touch, they are often the most time-consuming and costly. The survey team member should frame the conversation as an opportunity to give input and improve service. These surveys aim to understand the customer's experience, focusing on their overall impression of the organization and any specific challenges they may have encountered. Phone surveys are best suited to obtain specific details by utilizing follow-up questions.

Paper surveys can be quick and easy to complete while removing technology and time barriers, as they can be completed onsite and with just a pen. Due to a rising distrust in technology, some users will find a paper version to have increased anonymity. These surveys provide an opportunity for customers to give feedback directly after an interaction, offering real-time insights into their experiences. Another benefit to paper surveys is often increased participation; by removing the technology and timing barriers, the return rate of these surveys is often higher. It is effective to use this method during meetings such as town halls, "all staff" meetings, or team building.

Data collection does not end with survey responses. It's equally or more important for managers and supervisors to engage with customers face-to-face, before, during, and after service. Observing these moments provides invaluable perspectives, revealing times when processes break down or

STEP 1: EVALUATE

when the staff member needs more training. For example, a manager observing the building permit application process would note when customers seem confused over required documentation or inefficiencies in the process that cause delays.

Watch

In the next part of the data collection process, the executive leadership team needs to collect internal data. To fully understand the needs of the staff, those at the supervisor and below, the leadership team should begin by gathering firsthand information. We refer to this as the "watch" stage. A "day in the life" or "ride-along" approach, when a director spends a day working alongside a staff member, provides the leadership team with crucial insights. During these visits, leaders should focus on seeing the work through the eyes of front-line staff while also building a rapport with them. In the *watch* stage, remember to use your eyes, not your mouth. Don't try to fix any issues you or the staff may find. Just collect the data. During this stage, if the employee is willing to share their feelings about the process, listen and create a comfortable environment for them to share.

By spending time in the field observing their team's day-to-day activities, leaders can better appreciate the intricacy of the work and discover new ways to support it. For example, a city manager may be more supportive of extending timelines after spending the day with a code enforcement officer and witnessing the challenges of balancing regulatory requirements with community needs. Firsthand experience provides for more practical and supportive decision-making.

This step is the most contested by leaders. Many feel they are too busy and don't have the time to simply "watch." If you feel this way, we encourage you to reflect on your organization's mission statement and the priorities set by the board. Shadowing employees is critical to the evaluation process and to developing a solution-focused culture. Simon Sinek said it best in *Leaders Eat Last*: "Leaders who spend time shadowing their employees develop a firsthand appreciation of their workers' skills and challenges. This not only improves morale but also equips leaders with the knowledge to make more effective decisions."

Listen

Now that the leadership team has gathered firsthand information and begun to build rapport with the staff, the next step is to listen. This step is focused on understanding the perspectives of the team members themselves. These are the people on the front lines, interacting directly with customers and dealing with the organization's internal processes every day. Their insights are important and help identify what is working well and what needs improvement. Continuing follow-up interviews with staff should focus on their experiences, challenges, and ideas for making the organization more solution-focused.

When gathering input from team members, it's important to ask questions and invite honest and thorough responses. Examples may include the following:

- What do you think works well in your department?
- Can you tell me a story about when you were able to help a customer and they left happy even though they didn't get exactly what they asked for?"
- What do you feel gets in the way of customer satisfaction?
- What resources do you need to do your job better?
- What would make your life at work easier?
- Which policies do you find cumbersome, and why?

These questions are designed to help leaders perform a deep dive into the day-to-day realities of their work, highlighting both the successes and the frustrations they experience. By really listening to staff, leaders can identify patterns and systemic issues that may not be visible at higher levels.

Beyond interviews, organizing group sessions, often known as "round tables," where small groups of employees meet with senior leadership, provides an additional tool to gather insights. This option is less time-consuming than traditional one-on-one interviews and provides employees with the opportunity to re-iterate or add to the opinions of others. In these sessions, leaders must start by ensuring employees feel safe to speak their minds. It can be helpful to start the session off by engaging a team member who is supportive of the mission and outspoken. Leaders should continue to emphasize that these conversations are a judgment-free zone where there will be no retaliation for sharing honest feedback. This openness can help uncover hidden problems and innovative ideas for improvement.

For this part of the data collection process, it is critical that leaders adopt a learning mindset. This means resisting the urge to suggest improvements on the spot or to critique how work is being done. Instead, they should focus on asking open-ended questions like, "Can you tell me more about this challenge and how it affects your job?" or "What changes would you make?" The goal is to listen and learn, not to manage.

Assess

Once data has been collected from leadership, customers, and team members, it's time to bring the information together for exploration. This is typically done in an off-site meeting with the entire leadership team. It is important that each member of the leadership team has a voice in the discussion and that the team is unbiased when identifying trends, themes, and areas of overlap among the data. In our story, TJ

STEP 1: EVALUATE

encouraged Walter to tease out his idea to ensure that the team felt comfortable sharing their ideas, even if they were critical of TJ or the council. The separation of taking the team off-site facilitates free speech and removes the distractions of the normal workday.

During the workshop, leaders will detect patterns in the data. For example, if multiple departments report that a certain purchasing policy creates frustration, that's an obvious area for improvement. In the story of Clearview, the leadership team discovered a pattern that included a lack of empowerment after many employees complained about the chain of command. If team members consistently express a desire for more training or new tools, it highlights a need that can be addressed through proper budgeting. During this phase of the assessment, the team can decide on some *easy wins*; for example, if the majority of the administrative staff complain that the postage machine is out of date and causes them a headache, replacing the machine could be a quick and easy win for the management team. These "easy wins" are important in the change process because, simply put, change is hard. Getting a few easy wins early on not only ensures the staff knows you are listening to them but also buys trust that your actions align with the mission, values, and concept of being solution-focused.

The goal of this process is to find common areas of concern among employees and customers. However, reviewing an extensive collection of data can be overwhelming. A helpful tip is to pay more attention to the quality of the positive comments and quantity of the negative comments; you can never please everyone. By identifying these shared challenges, the leadership team can prioritize issues that will have the greatest impact on both employee satisfaction and customer service. Additionally, this process provides an opportunity to see and celebrate areas where the organization excels.

STEP 1: EVALUATE

While this analysis is critical, it's only the beginning of the transformation process. After the data has been evaluated and reviewed by the leadership team, set it aside for later. This information will become more valuable throughout the Engage and Empower stages of the solution-focused process. Rather than acting on this information, it is now time for the leadership team to focus on involving the rest of the organization in developing solutions.

By aligning the goals of the executive leadership team with the mission of the organization, watching the challenges of front-line staff, listening to employees' concerns, and assessing the customer experience, you are ready to create the foundation for building a solution-focused culture. This process requires a willingness to listen and learn, and a bit of patience. After developing a clear understanding of where the organization stands, leaders can move forward confidently and involve their team to ensure they are addressing the right problems in the most effective way. This approach not only improves customer experience, but also fosters a culture of ownership, innovation, and shared success, making it possible to transform even the most "no-centric" organization into a solution-focused one.

STEP ONE ACTIVITY

Ride-Alongs

Objective:
To provide leaders with a firsthand understanding of each division's roles, challenges, and contributions through direct observation and participation. This activity builds cross-functional empathy, enhances communication, and strengthens the leader's connection to the team's daily work.

Materials Needed:
-Ride-along schedule
-Notebook for the leader to take notes and document insights
-Prepared list of discussion prompts or questions

Time Needed:
A half-day per division, scheduled over the course of several weeks, depending on the organization's size.

Steps:
1. Preparation and Scheduling (1 week before)

- Coordinate with division heads to schedule the leader's ride-along for each division, ensuring the timing works for both the leader and the team.
- Brief team members on the purpose of the ride-along, emphasizing that it is an opportunity for open dialogue, understanding, and potential collaboration.
- Provide the leader with an outline of each division's functions and any specific questions to guide the observation (e.g., key workflows, common challenges, or unique aspects of the team's work).

2. Kick-Off Discussion with Each Division (15-20 minutes at start of each day)
- Begin each ride-along with a brief discussion led by the division head, explaining their team's role, recent accomplishments, and current challenges.
- Allow team members to share their perspectives, ask questions, and set any expectations for the day.
- Encourage an open, informal tone to foster genuine exchanges and help the leader gain insight into the team's experiences.

3. Hands-On Observation and Engagement (3-4 hours)
- The leader should shadow different team members, observing their workflows, tools, and daily routines.
- Encourage the leader to ask questions and, when possible, assist with tasks to gain a better appreciation of the team's work.
- Focus on understanding how the division contributes to the organization's goals, noting any inefficiencies, pain points, or standout practices.

4. Informal Check-Ins Throughout the Day
- During breaks or downtime, the leader should initiate informal discussions with team members, encouraging them

to share insights on what they enjoy about their roles, improvements they would suggest, and how they view their contribution to the organization's mission.
-Record feedback on areas such as collaboration, resource needs, and cross-divisional dependencies.

5. Reflection and Feedback Session (20-30 minutes at end of each day)
-Conclude each ride-along with a feedback session where the leader shares initial reflections and asks for any final thoughts from the team.
-Use this time to discuss any immediate takeaways and ideas for potential improvements or future collaborations.
-Express appreciation for the team's openness and contributions.

6. Post-Ride-Along Debrief (following all ride-alongs)
-After completing ride-alongs with each division, the leader should compile insights and recommendations, identifying themes and specific areas for improvement or resource allocation.
-Organize a team meeting or presentation to share high-level findings with the entire organization, celebrating strengths and proposing next steps to address common challenges or leverage best practices.

Summary:
Leadership ride-alongs foster a deeper understanding between divisions and organizational leaders, building empathy and informed decision-making. This experience promotes transparency, team morale, and cross-functional alignment, as the leader gains insight into each division's unique contributions and the organization gains a leader more connected to and invested in their team's daily successes and challenges.

STEP 2: ESTABLISH

Core values are the DNA of an organization's culture. These values define what an organization stands for, how it operates, and how it expects its employees to behave. Core values ensure consistency in actions throughout the organization. They also provide a set of guidelines that ensure that employees understand what the organization will and won't do. These values are, as described by Darrel in the story, the box around a field in which the employees are free to play as long as they don't get outside of the box.

Developing and reinforcing core values takes considerable time and effort, but the payoff is a healthy organization that can weather change and thrive in the face of challenges.

In the preceding fable, the story of Clearview started with an organization where the governing body knew there was a problem but had not identified what the problem was, or, more importantly, *how* to go about fixing it. To address the problem, they hired a new chief administrative officer. The new manager, TJ Strong, assessed the operations of the city and determined that the challenge in the organization was culture-based. Following his initial assessment of the staff and an existing strategic plan, TJ set in motion a review of the existing strategic plan, the development of a mission statement, and the establishment of core values, all focused on addressing a culture of "no."

If your organization does not have a mission or vision statement, you should first develop these statements. There are many books that cover this topic, such as *The Path – Creating Your Mission Statements for Work and Life* by Laurie Beth Jones.

The creation and implementation of core values is not a one-size-fits-all process. We will provide evidence-based practices and tips, but this process involves individualized reflection, discussion, connection, and reinforcement. Every organization's journey to success is unique, but one constant is the need for across-the-board involvement. To succeed, an organization must engage its governing board, executive leadership, and staff, ensuring collaboration and alignment across the entire company.

As mentioned in Step 1, start by analyzing the existing culture and priorities of leadership. Successfully completing the Align step is vital at this point, as each value must reflect and support the organization's overall mission. Once you have ensured the support of the board and aligned the leadership team, you should begin involving staff in establishing organizational core values.

Reflect

An organization's core values should reflect the mission statement. It's essential to connect each value to the employee's everyday responsibilities; abstract values may be disregarded or lose significance. Values like transparency are more likely to be embraced by staff because they can clearly understand the direct relation to their work.

Additionally, core values should reflect the entire organization, not just the leadership team. Engaging employees in this process is critical for developing individual ownership.

STEP 2: ESTABLISH

The establishment of core values should coincide with the establishment of an employee committee, often referred to as a *cross-functional team* or *process-improvement team* (PIT).

The PIT, with the assistance of the facilitator, will collect input from their coworkers, brainstorm and vet ideas, create and define the values, and ultimately present these ideas for adoption to the leadership team. The PIT will continue as the advocate for the adoption and implementation of the core values moving forward.

The team developing your core values should be as diverse as the organization; this includes age, ethnicity, and gender. Additionally, this team should include representation from each department, a mix of front-line staff and management, as well as service workers and professionals. While forming your process improvement team, be sure to invite all influential leaders to participate. This may include long-time staff members, popular teammates, union leadership, or even disgruntled employees. Be sure to choose a facilitator skilled in seeking input from all, keeping the team focused and capable of leading the group to a solution, not forcing their solution on the team. When employees at all levels feel a sense of ownership, the values become more than just words—they transform into principles that guide everyday behavior and guarantee outcomes aligned with the company's mission.

Discuss

There may be many principles you want to instill in your organization. But it's best to focus on a small set of core values that are critical to the company's mission. Too many values weaken their importance and make it harder for employees to internalize them. Aim for three to five core values that are non-negotiable.

The employee team will need to meet several times to discuss potential values. Keep the team to a manageable size or split it into several smaller groups with additional facilitators; facilitating conversations about each value is crucial. Employees should be able to express how these values align with the company's mission, influence their work routines, and affect the customers they serve. We see this connection in Clearview's off-site meeting, where the finance director discusses how the core value of transparency directly connects to the everyday operations of the finance department. The ability for the values to resonate with all the departments is another reason to ensure the team is a cross-section of your organization.

Tips for creating values:

- Use simple, actionable language.
- Make the values easy to understand and remember.
- Try to avoid vague buzzwords that lack substance.
- Focus on behavioral values that guide day-to-day actions.

While discussing values and the language associated, it can be helpful to use terms that are easily associated. Acronyms, alliteration, and mnemonics are effective strategies for making your set of values more memorable. In the Clearview story, they developed the acronym TRAITS. Another example would be the Kraft-Heinz Company core values of WIN: "Work as a team, inspire excellence, navigate our future."

Staff will remember stories better than ambiguous concepts. While discussing these concepts, try to use real-life examples to illustrate how the core values play out in the workplace. We see this in the story of Clearview when, in chapter 9, the police chief suggests Integrity and explains how this value connects to the everyday life of a police officer. Be sure to highlight employees or teams who represent the values in action. Later in the process, share these stories in

STEP 2: ESTABLISH

meetings, newsletters, and other organizational communications.

Communicate

Once your core values are well-defined, the next step is to clearly and consistently communicate these values across the organization. Your organization's success in changing its culture hinges on how well employees understand and embrace the new values.

The communication process should begin before the hiring process. Employees are increasingly seeking organizations whose values echo their own. A strong values-driven culture can help attract top talent. Creating a page on your outward-facing website that highlights the organization's core values is a great way to differentiate yourself from competitors in a tough labor market. Candidates should be introduced to the core values during the application process. A great way to do this is by highlighting these values in the Organizational Summary section of the job description.

When an applicant is selected for an interview, you must determine whether the candidate aligns with the organization's core values. Hiring decisions should be based not only on technical skills but also on cultural fit. During the interview process, we suggest using behavioral interviewing techniques with questions that incorporate your core values. For example, an organization that defined *adaptability* as a core value may ask the candidate to tell a story about a time when they worked for an organization undergoing significant organizational change and explain how they coped with the change. Employees who resonate with the company's core values are more likely to contribute positively to the culture. This is especially crucial when hiring members of the executive leadership team.

It is vital that the process continues after the candidate has been selected. Onboarding is the opportune time to explain the significance of the values and how they influence daily operations, expectations for employee behavior, and customer interactions. While onboarding is often led by human resources, senior leaders should continue the discussion of core values by giving real-world examples of employee and organizational behavior that have directly led to success. This early exposure helps set expectations for how employees should act and make decisions.

Reinforce

The true challenge comes in reinforcing core values over time. Organizational culture shifts gradually, and instilling core values requires continual effort.

Leadership must be the champion of the organization's core values. The executive team must regularly communicate and reinforce the importance of these values during "all staff" meetings, when making decisions, and by personal example. Employees take cues from their leaders, so it is essential for managers and executives to consistently model the core values. If *collaboration* is a value, leaders should actively seek input from their teams and facilitate open communication. If *innovation* is a core value, leadership should encourage and reward risk-taking and creative problem-solving. When leaders visibly embody the values, employees are more likely to follow suit.

Much like core values are an essential part of evaluating a candidate for hire, these values must also be a part of the process that determines if an employee is promoted or stays with the organization. Integrating core values into performance reviews and promotion criteria encourages managers to direct these conversations toward organizational values rather than just technical expertise. An organization with *alignment* in its values will assess employees not only on what they achieve but also on how they achieve it. Tying promotions and evaluations to core values ensures that the behav-

STEP 2: ESTABLISH

iors rewarded align with the organization's values and facilitates proper feedback or coaching when an employee's behavior is inconsistent with those values.

Positive reinforcement of the core values should also occur outside formal evaluations and promotions. Make sure you publicly recognize employees who live the values. Public recognition doesn't have to be face-to-face; company websites and social media pages are great alternatives to public meetings. This can be done less formally in a department where peers recognize one another, or more formally through awards programs such as Employee of the Month or MVP programs. The name of the program will vary from organization to organization. What is important is that these awards are distributed throughout the year and are designed to celebrate those who embody the organization's core values. The public recognition, prize, and clarity will inspire others to follow suit.

Core values are more than just words on a wall. They serve as the foundation for long-term success. When core values are deeply ingrained in the culture, they guide decision-making, foster engagement, and drive alignment across the organization.

STEP TWO ACTIVITY

Discover Your Values

Objective:

To collaboratively define the core values that represent the beliefs and principles guiding the organization's behaviors, decisions, and mission.

Materials Needed:
-Whiteboard or large flipchart
-Markers
-Sticky notes or index cards
-Pens for each participant
-Core Values Examples handout

Time Needed:

Approximately 60-90 minutes, depending on group size and discussion depth

STEP TWO ACTIVITY

Steps:

1. Set the Stage (5-10 minutes)
-Begin by explaining the purpose of the activity: to establish a set of shared core values that will guide the organization's culture, decisions, and behaviors.
-Briefly discuss why core values are important and share examples of other organizations' core values to inspire thinking.

2. Reflect on Personal Values (10 minutes)
-Ask each participant to reflect on the values they personally feel are most important in a workplace.
-Encourage them to think about what principles they believe guide their everyday actions.
-Suggest they think about the behaviors of a valued teammate.
-Have them write down 3-5 values on individual sticky notes or index cards.

3. Share and Discuss (10-15 minutes)
-Ask each participant to share their values with the group, placing each sticky note on the whiteboard or flipchart.
-As values are shared, group similar values together. For example, values like "integrity" and "honesty" should be clustered together.
-Discuss any differences and clarify meanings as needed to ensure everyone has a shared understanding.

4. Identify Themes and Prioritize (15-20 minutes)
-After all values are shared, identify any emerging themes by examining the clustered values.
-Use consensus or voting to prioritize 5-7 values that the team feels best represent the organization's core beliefs.

STEP TWO ACTIVITY

-Encourage participants to choose values that are authentic, unique, and meaningful to the organization's identity and goals.

5. Define Each Value (15-20 minutes)
-For each selected value, discuss as a group what this value looks like in action.
Answer questions such as the following:
—What behaviors would reflect this value?
—How does this value align with the organization's mission?
—How can this value help guide decision-making?
-Capture the descriptions of each core value, adding a sentence or two that clearly defines what each value means to the organization.

6. Discuss Implementation and Accountability (10-15 minutes)
-Lead a discussion on how the team will uphold these values across the organization.
Consider questions like the following:
—How will we recognize or reward behaviors aligned with these values?
—How will we ensure accountability for living up to these values?
This conversation will help set the foundation for embedding the core values into the organization's culture.

7. Finalize and Reflect (10 minutes)
-Review the final list of core values and definitions with the group.
-Reflect on how these values align with the organization's mission and vision.
-Conclude by emphasizing the importance of each leader modeling these values.

STEP TWO ACTIVITY

Summary:
By the end of this activity, your leadership team will have a clearly defined set of core values that represent the organization's core beliefs. These values will serve as guiding principles for decision-making, culture building, and organizational behavior.

STEP 3: EXPLAIN

The next step in creating a solution-focused culture is explaining the goals of the organization to your staff. After evaluating the organization's needs and establishing core values, it's time to bring those findings into clear, actionable focus. Without clearly articulated goals, even the most dedicated team can struggle to "reach the endzone," as Darnell would say.

The goals of an organization act as the path between a mission statement and reality. If core values define who you are as an organization, goals define where you are going. However, simply setting goals at the executive level is not enough. These goals must be communicated effectively and repeatedly so everyone understands their role in achieving them.

Connection

Organizational goals do not exist in a vacuum. To be effective, they must be tied back to the mission and core values established earlier. When employees see that the goals align with the values of the organization, they'll be more motivated to work toward them. For example, if one of your core values is *innovation*, then your goals should not only be about growth but also about creativity and new ideas.

Shared goals strengthen trust between the employees and leadership. Staff members want to know that the goals they are working toward are consistent with the mission and values that guide the organization. By reinforcing this connection, the organization demonstrates integrity and strengthens employee engagement.

Clarity

When developing a solution-focused culture, the way goals are communicated is just as important as the goals themselves. When goals are communicated clearly and effectively, staff can see the bigger picture. They understand not only what they are working toward but why it matters. And when they understand this, they are more likely to be creative in finding solutions that move the organization forward.

When employees don't have a clear sense of the organization's objectives, confusion and disengagement can set in. Alternatively, when they understand how their daily work contributes to the mission, it creates purpose, motivation, and a sense of accomplishment. All staff members should be able to articulate, in simple terms, the primary goals of the organization without having to remember corporate jargon or vague, nonsensical statements. Aim for simplicity without sacrificing the integrity of the goal.

To achieve clear goals, use the SMART goals method. All goals must be specific, measurable, attainable, relevant, and time-bound (SMART). This framework not only provides clarity but also offers a practical guide to breaking down larger goals into manageable tasks. A solution-focused team may decide they need to improve customer satisfaction. To make this into a SMART goal, the leader should break the task down by asking the following questions: How much do we want to increase satisfaction? Can we measure this task? Is the specific number we wish to achieve attainable for this team? Is customer satis-faction relevant to all members of this team? How much time does the team have to accomplish this goal?

For this example, if the leadership team wants to increase satisfaction, they must *specify* the mechanism for measuring the outcome, such as a percentage or number. They can *measure* this goal utilizing the survey tools discussed in step one, *attain* this through additional training, make it *relevant* to everyone by explaining the concept of external and internal customers, and provide an appropriate *time* frame. The finalized SMART goal is as follows:

The City of Clearview will increase customer satisfaction by 20% over the next six months, as measured by post-engagement customer satisfaction survey ratings. The clearer the goal, the easier it is for staff to meet it.

How you communicate goals will vary depending on your audience. When deciding how to communicate your goals to the variety of groups you will experience in any organization, you must first consider questions such as the following:

- What do I know about this team?
- Is their leader new to the organization?
- Have they experienced significant organizational trauma?
- As a team, are they high performing or low?
- Is the majority of staff long-term employees or newer hires?

All of these factors impact how the team receives your message. When work groups are composed of new leaders or mostly new staff, they tend to ask more questions and are free from the constraints of past failures, but they've also had fewer experiences to fully understand how the organizational goal ties into the mission and values. Teams that have been through organizational traumas have a tendency to be wary of new ideas and may outright refuse; you'll need to take extra time and care with these teams to ensure they understand that things will be different this time. High-performing teams should be celebrated and see goals as a way to articulate their success clearly. They will likely embrace changes that they believe will improve their performance. Conversely, low-performing teams tend to provide excuses and be contrary. Be sure to listen first, and then ensure they know you believe in them and will provide them with the tools necessary for success. Take your time when communicating, and you'll start to develop a network of employees who will champion the organization's goals even when you are not around.

Different teams within the organization will need different levels of detail and emphasis. For example:

-Senior management: Communicate strategic goals in terms of mission and vision, long-term impact to the organization, and metrics. This group will benefit from presentations, executive summaries, and strategic plan review sessions.

-Middle management: Translate strategic goals into actionable projects. Communicate through meetings, project management tools, and leadership discussions, emphasizing accountability and departmental objectives.

-Frontline employees: Break down goals into daily tasks and operational processes. Use language that is relatable, focusing on how these tasks contribute to the mission and overall organizational goals.

Trackable

Now that the goals have been clearly communicated, the next step is to make them actionable. This means breaking

STEP 3: EXPLAIN

them down into smaller, trackable objectives for individuals and teams. Everyone should have a clear understanding of what success looks like and how their progress will be measured. Applying the SMART goal highlighted earlier to a frontline customer service team member could include improving the average customer satisfaction score from 3 to 4 and working with the service team to review the survey data.

In a solution-focused culture, we understand the need for change, including course correction. Tracking isn't just about numbers; it's also about learning. What's working? What needs to change? How can you be more effective in ensuring your team reaches each milestone? Managers should review goals with their staff no less than quarterly to ensure they are on track, and if not, learn from the disruption.

In our customer service example, the manager reviews survey data with the team every two weeks based on billing cycles. After reviewing multiple months of survey data with the customer service team, the manager addresses the lack of progress and determines the team has not had sufficient training on de-escalation. When an angry customer comes to the office, it takes an excessive amount of time and impacts the overall experience for all customers. Continuing to focus on the goal, the manager implements a de-escalation policy and schedules training for frontline staff. Additionally, to ensure future milestones are met, the manager observes each staff member to provide instant, actionable feedback should an escalation occur. This is one piece of a feedback loop. Feedback is also provided through a more formal process during employee performance reviews and less directly in settings such as roundtable meetings, where employees are invited to give suggestions on how the organization can improve. By embedding a feedback loop into the goal-tracking process, you're promoting a culture of continuous improvement. This will empower staff to adapt and refine their approach, contributing to a dynamic and solution-focused culture.

STEP 3: EXPLAIN

Explaining organizational goals to your staff is not a one-time event; it's an ongoing conversation. Clarity, alignment with core values, engagement in the goal-setting process, and tailoring communication to different levels of the organization are all essential elements in building a solution-focused culture.

In the next step, we'll explore how to foster accountability throughout the organization, ensuring that goals are not only understood but also achieved in a sustainable, collaborative manner.

STEP THREE ACTIVITY

Values in Action Storytelling

Objective:

To help employees connect with organizational values through real-life examples and storytelling, illustrating how these values shape the company culture and guide daily actions.

Materials Needed:

-Whiteboard or flipchart
-Markers
-Printed handouts of the organizational values
-Notecards or sticky notes
-Pens for each participant

Time Needed:

Approximately 45-60 minutes

STEP THREE ACTIVITY

Steps:
1. Introduction to Values (5-10 minutes)
-Begin by introducing each of the organization's values and explaining that this session will involve sharing stories about these values in action.
-Emphasize how values are brought to life through real behaviors and decisions, having meaningful impact within the organization.

2. Personal Reflection and Story Preparation (10 minutes)
-Give employees a few minutes to think of a time when they or someone else demonstrated one of the organizational values in a meaningful way.
-Ask them to write a brief description of this story on a notecard or sticky note, keeping in mind questions like the following:
—What happened?
—How was the value demonstrated?
—What impact did this have on the team, client, or company?

3. Small Group Story Sharing (15-20 minutes)
-Divide employees into small groups of 3-5 and invite each person to share their story with the group.
-Encourage employees to listen actively and ask questions, aiming to draw out the significance of the values in each story.

4. Group Highlights (10-15 minutes)
-Ask each group to select one or two stories they found especially inspiring or illustrative of a core value to share with the larger group.
-Each small group presents these stories, emphasizing how the value was shown and its positive impact on the team or company.

STEP THREE ACTIVITY

5. Reflect on Values in Practice (5 minutes)
-Conclude by encouraging participants to think of ways they can bring these values to life in their roles.
-Consider adding a visual element, such as posting the stories in a common area or creating a "Values in Action" bulletin board to highlight these examples regularly.

Summary:
This storytelling activity allows employees to see the organizational values as real, practical, and achievable behaviors rather than abstract concepts. Sharing stories fosters a sense of connection, reinforces a positive culture, and encourages employees to embody the values in their own work.

STEP 4: ENGAGE

Success isn't driven from the top down in a solution-focused culture. It's a team effort where everyone actively contributes to identifying challenges and finding solutions. The ability to engage your team in this process nurtures innovation and builds ownership.

Safety

"Psychological safety is a condition in which you feel included, safe to learn, safe to contribute, and safe to challenge the status quo—all without fear of being embarrassed, marginalized, or punished in some way," states Timothy R. Clark, author of *The 4 Stages of Psychological Safety: Defining the Path to Inclusion and Innovation*. Before your team can effectively contribute to a solution, they need to feel safe doing so.

Leaders set the tone for the entire organization. If team members feel that their ideas will be dismissed, harshly judged, or even worse, ostracized for contributing their perspectives, they will not participate freely. To encourage such participation, leaders must create safety by demonstrating active listening, showing appreciation for diverse perspectives, and providing constructive feedback.

STEP 4: ENGAGE

Additional tips for creating psychological safety include the following:

Vulnerability: Vulnerability is a key component of leadership. A leader who admits their mistakes will build psychological safety expeditiously.

Transparency: Invite feedback and create space for honest discussion, such as workshops, brainstorming meetings, or open forums, where the sole intent of the meeting is for staff to share their ideas.

Call for questions: Show the team that asking questions is not a sign of weakness or lack of knowledge but instead a key part of the process. Often, early on, leaders must make the call for questions or assign a team member to be the dissenter in order to incite additional questions.

Celebrate progress: Sometimes solutions may not work as planned. By celebrating the effort behind an attempt, employees are motivated to continue work on the next iteration.

Source vs. Symptom

For your team to engage in meaningful problem-solving, they must learn to dig deep to uncover the true source of the problem. This involves shifting from a reactive mentality to a proactive approach that addresses the underlying causes. We saw this play out in the story of Clearview. When TJ called the customer who was complaining about customer service, he learned that the issue was as much or more about the software used by the city as it was about the employee's attitude. In this example, both were a problem, but they stemmed from the source issue of having software that served as a roadblock to service, resulting in a frustrated employee and customer.

STEP 4: ENGAGE

At the end of the book, we saw the same employee loving her ability to serve the customers better because the software (source problem) was replaced.

If TJ had simply replaced the employee, the source would have remained, and the problems would have continued.

Engaging your team in effective solution development often hits a roadblock: focusing only on immediate, surface-level symptoms rather than digging deeper to address the underlying root causes. The solution to this challenge is to train your team to distinguish between the symptom of an issue and its true source. While addressing symptoms may provide temporary relief, it's solving the underlying cause or source that leads to lasting success.

Symptoms are the visible signs of a problem. They're what your team experiences—missed deadlines, customer complaints, or roadblocks. Symptoms are plain to see but can be misleading, often tempting teams to implement quick fixes that fail to address the root cause.

Sources, on the other hand, are the deeper, often less obvious, causes behind those symptoms. For example, missed deadlines might be a symptom, but the source could be poor communication, inefficient processes, or unclear expectations. If your team focuses only on the symptom—rushing to meet deadlines without addressing the cause—they'll likely find themselves in the same position down the road.

Techniques to foster this mindset:

The 5 Whys technique: Simple but effective, ask, "Why?" five times to reveal all the layers of a problem. By asking, "Why?" repeatedly, the team can move beyond the initial symptom and uncover the source.[1]

---

1. Ohno, Taiichi. *Toyota Production System: Beyond Large-Scale*

STEP 4: ENGAGE

Process mapping: Visually map out the entire process where the issue occurs, including a workflow diagram, a customer journey map, or supply chain charts. The team analyzes the steps, handoffs, and potential breakdowns to pinpoint where failure occurs and discern the source program.

Fishbone diagram (Ishikawa diagram): Visualize symptoms broken down into categories with the head of the fish labeled as the problem and the bones branching off the spine representing major causes.[2]

Building a solution-focused culture means making these approaches to problem-solving part of the organization's DNA. Incorporating after-action meetings as a common practice provides routine feedback on how to best approach challenging problems. During after-action meetings, managers are given the opportunity to learn about the needs of staff, which may include tools, training, or equipment. On the other side, these meetings provide a perfect opportunity to reinforce the efforts of the team. Use these meetings as an opportunity to publicly recognize staff for going beyond the symptoms to discover lasting solutions, and you can expect to see these behaviors become a regular practice.

Teams

Once a safe environment is established and the source versus symptom mindset has been implemented, the next step is to form cross-departmental teams. Departmental silos inhibit the flow of ideas across the organization. To overcome this, cross-department collaboration through well-structured process improvement teams must be utilized. You may recall

---

Production. Productivity Press, 1988.
2. Ishikawa, Kaoru. *Guide to Quality Control.* Asian Productivity Organization, 1986.

in Step 2, we discussed a process improvement team set up for the purpose of developing core values, but those same principles apply to developing teams to solve any problem. Bringing together teams from different parts of the organization allows for the exchange of diverse views, leading to more inclusive and actionable solutions.

For example, if your organization is facing a customer service issue, involve not just the customer support team but also marketing, product development, and operations. These departments may uncover insights that the customer service team alone would not have considered. Cross-functional brainstorming sessions or project teams can generate more comprehensive solutions.

Subject Matter Experts

In a solution-focused culture, knowledge-sharing is crucial for building a stronger, more adaptable organization. Certain employees hold specialized knowledge in particular areas; these individuals are known as subject matter experts (SMEs). In Clearview, examples of SMEs include Carol in Utility Billing, Officer Simmons, and Jim Adams in Facility Maintenance. SMEs can include technical experts such as engineers, process specialists, or veterans with years of experience. These people understand specific systems, technologies, regulations, or workflows better than anyone else in the organization. An SME's expertise allows the team to avoid common pitfalls, recognizes hidden opportunities, and provides clarity on technical or specialized challenges. Tapping into their expertise ensures more informed decision-making and accelerates the team's ability to craft actionable solutions.

Subject matter experts are often busy with their regular responsibilities, so it's important to use their time wisely. Be clear about what you need from them and respect their availability. When inviting them to contribute, ensure they know the challenges the team is facing and how they can be helpful.

Be mindful of the balance; the goal is not to delegate all problem-solving to your SMEs, but to use their expertise as a tool in the problem-solving process.

A common mistake leaders make after recognizing an SME is bringing them into the process too late, after decisions have already been made, or when the team is deep into problem-solving. By being part of the initial discussions, SMEs can help define the problem more clearly and provide crucial context.

Ownership

The term *buy-in* commonly describes a situation where an employee is engaged with an idea proposed by leadership, similar to how one might buy stock in a publicly traded company. One share of Coca-Cola stock might get you a vote, but you aren't overly invested in the decisions made by the company. But if you own the company, whether a small business or a controlling share of a large corporation, you are heavily invested in the outcome of each decision. Similarly, one of the most effective ways to engage employees in developing solutions is to give them ownership over specific initiatives. When individuals are entrusted with leading a project or solving a particular challenge, they feel more empowered and responsible for the outcome.

This doesn't give leaders a free pass to delegate and walk away. They need to provide the necessary support and resources while also allowing team members to take the lead in decision-making and problem-solving. Giving staff autonomy not only fosters innovation but also increases accountability and personal investment.

A solution-focused culture is built on the idea that every employee has the potential to contribute to the organization's success. By engaging your team in developing solutions, you not only tap into their diverse skills and perspectives but also

STEP 4: ENGAGE

create a deeper sense of ownership and commitment. In the next step, we'll discuss how to foster accountability and ensure that the solutions developed by your team are implemented and sustained over the long term.

STEP FOUR ACTIVITY

Ownership Workshop

Objective:
To encourage employees to take greater ownership of their day-to-day responsibilities by identifying areas where they can make decisions, initiate improvements, and take proactive steps within their roles. This activity helps employees feel empowered, trusted, and motivated to contribute more effectively to the organization's goals.

Materials Needed:
- Whiteboard or flipchart
- Markers
- Sticky notes or index cards
- Pens for each participant

Time Needed:
Approximately 60-75 minutes

STEP FOUR ACTIVITY

Steps

1. Define Ownership and Its Benefits (10 minutes)
-Begin by introducing the concept of ownership in the workplace, explaining how it empowers employees to take initiative, make decisions, and feel more accountable for their work.
-Discuss the benefits of ownership, such as increased job satisfaction, creativity, and a greater impact on the organization's success.
-Encourage employees to see ownership as a way to influence their own roles and drive positive changes within the organization.

2. Identify Current Ownership Areas (10 minutes)
-Ask each employee to reflect on their current role and write down areas where they feel they already have ownership or decision-making power.
-Invite a few volunteers to share their examples, noting any patterns on a whiteboard or flipchart.
-This reflection helps employees see where they are already empowered, setting the stage to identify areas for greater ownership.

3. Find Opportunities for Increased Ownership (10-15 minutes)
-Ask employees to think of areas in their roles where they would like more responsibility, influence, or autonomy.
-Instruct them to write each area on a sticky note or index card, then place these ideas on the whiteboard or a designated space.
-As a group, review these ideas to identify common themes or frequently mentioned areas, helping employees see shared goals and opportunities.

STEP FOUR ACTIVITY

4. Small Group Brainstorming on Ownership Actions (15-20 minutes)

-Divide employees into small groups and assign each group one or two of the top areas identified.

-Instruct each group to brainstorm specific actions employees can take to increase ownership in that area, asking them to consider the following:

—Steps they can take independently or as a team

—Decisions they could make without additional approvals

—Ways to initiate or improve processes

-Each group should document their ideas and be ready to share them with the larger group.

5. Group Presentation and Ownership Commitments (10-15 minutes)

-Have each group present their action ideas to the larger team, explaining how they envision taking ownership in specific areas.

-After each presentation, allow for group discussion to refine ideas or offer additional suggestions.

-Encourage each participant to select at least one action item they feel they can implement in their role and write it down as their personal ownership commitment.

6. Follow-Up and Accountability (5-10 minutes)

-Conclude by encouraging employees to check in regularly with their supervisor or team about their ownership actions. -Supervisors should provide guidance and recognize efforts to reinforce this ownership culture.

-Suggest setting up monthly or quarterly follow-ups for employees to share successes, challenges, and additional ideas for building ownership in their work.

STEP FOUR ACTIVITY

Summary:
This workshop enables employees to identify and commit to areas where they can take greater ownership in their day-to-day roles. By giving employees the tools and confidence to make decisions, initiate improvements, and feel accountable for their contributions, this activity builds a culture of empowerment, initiative, and engagement across the organization.

STEP 5: EMPOWER

Leadership isn't about making top-down decisions; it's about empowering every employee in the organization to take ownership and find solutions. We prioritize the empowerment of individuals rather than the team as a unit because empowerment focuses on developing a person's decision-making skills and confidence. Allowing employees to make choices fosters self-assurance and capability while also expediting problem-solving, nurturing innovation, and enhancing overall employee engagement.

In many struggling organizations, decisions are concentrated at the top, with employees relying heavily on managers for direction. This centralization can lead to roadblocks, delayed responses to issues, and an overall lack of accountability from employees. When employees feel unable to make basic decisions related to their work, they often defer responsibility or disengage from problem-solving entirely. When employees feel empowered to make decisions and find solutions, it creates a more dynamic and agile organization. Empowerment shifts the mindset from dependency to autonomy, where every employee sees themselves as an active participant in the organization's success.

STEP 5: EMPOWER

Trust is the foundation of empowerment. Leaders must trust their employees to make decisions, and employees must trust that their leaders will support them when they take action. For many leaders, this shift from giving specific directions to empowering individual employees can be challenging. This shift requires a substantial change in mindset: leaders must move from being the problem-solvers to trusting their teams to take the needed action. In order to create this trust and empower employees, leaders need to provide clear boundaries, create a supportive environment, and ensure staff members have all the necessary tools.

Clear Boundaries

Empowerment does not equate to giving employees *free rein* to do whatever they want. It actually requires well-defined boundaries and expectations. Employees must understand the goals of the organization, their role within it, and the limits within which they can make decisions. We cover the explanation of organizational goals in Step 3; when setting boundaries, it is important to remember that "explaining the goals" is an ongoing step. Leaders must reinforce what each employee is responsible for and how these tasks align with the organization's goals.

Empowerment works best when employees have flexibility and autonomy. Whether it's the ability to adjust processes, offer discounts, or choose tools, the boundaries should be straightforward but provide enough room for independent action.

One way to ensure clear boundaries is to create procedures that specify the areas where employees should make decisions on their own, when they need to seek supervisory input, or areas that are strictly for the executive team or governing body. Having a structured approach to decision-making allows employees to confidently take action while

STEP 5: EMPOWER

ensuring alignment with larger goals and easing management's worries.

Environment

Empowered employees are solution focused: they don't just point out problems; they take steps to fix them. As a leader, you must not only provide your employees with the physical tools to complete the job but also an environment that is conducive to this behavior. A solution-focused culture thrives when the environment encourages critical thinking, supports risk-taking, and celebrates initiative.

Critical thinking allows employees to analyze problems deeply, question assumptions, and develop innovative solutions. Leaders can foster this by asking thought-provoking questions and allowing time for reflection. Further, it enables employees to apply their insights with confidence and autonomy.

Risk-taking is essential for innovation, but it requires a supportive environment where failure is viewed as a learning opportunity. Leaders should first establish clear areas where it is OK and actually encouraged to take risks, then promote a safe-to-fail culture, frame mistakes as part of the growth process, and reward courageous actions. This encourages employees to experiment with new ideas without fear, driving progress and creative problem-solving.

Celebrating initiative is crucial to empowerment. Employees must feel trusted to take ownership and act independently. Recognizing and rewarding their contributions builds confidence and inspires others to follow suit. When an organization rewards risk-taking and initiative, it becomes more agile and adaptable, setting the stage for a thriving solution-focused culture.

Empowerment doesn't mean employees work in isolation. In fact, one of the most impactful ways to empower individuals is to encourage peer support and collaboration. By creating an environment where critical thinking and risk-taking are celebrated, it becomes easy for employees to ask for help or share ideas at regular team meetings and informal discussion groups. Communication platforms like Teams and Slack allow employees to develop relationships with one another and feel supported and engaged. Additionally, when leadership encourages employees from different departments or teams to collaborate on solutions, these cross-functional teams will not only broaden individual perspectives but will also impart a deeper understanding of the organization. This type of collaboration also helps to build a more cohesive organization where employees feel empowered to leverage the expertise of their peers. When employees rely on each other for advice, guidance, and feedback, they are more likely to feel confident in their decisions.

Tools

Empowering employees without providing the necessary tools and resources sets them up for failure, undermining both their confidence and the organization's goals. To fully empower employees, leaders must ensure they have access to the best information, support, and tools to make informed decisions and implement the solution.

Transparency in sharing current performance, customer feedback, and relevant trends equip individuals to act strategically rather than reactively. You must make it easy for employees to access this information and be sure they understand how it applies to their role.

It can be easy for leaders to forget that our employees are the best tools in our toolbox. Providing staff with ongoing support through training, mentorship, and guidance ensures that employees continue to develop the skills and knowledge needed to confidently and consistently contribute innovative solutions.

Whether it's a communication platform that streamlines

STEP 5: EMPOWER

collaboration, tablets that track work orders on the go, or robotic lawnmowers, the right technology allows employees to execute their responsibilities efficiently. Without the right tools, employees become frustrated and lose their ability to take initiative, but when employees feel well-equipped, empowered decision-making becomes the norm.

In the story of Clearview, we saw just how frustrated employees like Carol, Jim, and Angie were when they felt like they could not solve the customers' problems. They all had the answers, but policy, hierarchy, and bureaucracy were killing innovation. When we create clear guidelines and empower our employees, problems that can be solved will be solved at the lowest levels, leaving leadership to work on achieving the vision and mission of the organization.

Empowering individual employees to make decisions and find solutions is the foundation of a solution-focused culture. It moves the organization from a reactive state, where problems are escalated up the chain, to a proactive state, where everyone is capable of taking action.

By clearly defining boundaries, fostering a solution-oriented mindset, providing the necessary tools, and encouraging peer collaboration, you will create an environment where employees are not only empowered to solve problems but are motivated to contribute to the organization's success.

STEP FIVE ACTIVITY

Needs Discussion

Objective:
To provide supervisors with a structured approach to understanding and addressing the current needs of their employees. This activity encourages open, one-on-one conversations that allow employees to share their needs and challenges, while supervisors who have not previously allowed their employees to make decisions they are competent enough to make learn how to best support and empower their employees for success.

Materials Needed:
-Discussion guide for supervisors (optional, with example questions)
-Notebook or tablet for each supervisor to take notes
-Quiet, comfortable meeting space for one-on-one conversations
-Whiteboard or flipchart for group reflection after the one-on-one discussions

STEP FIVE ACTIVITY

Time Needed:
60-90 minutes, including group reflection and wrap-up

Steps:
1. Preparation and Overview (10-15 minutes)
-Begin with a brief group discussion among supervisors to introduce the purpose of the activity. (Emphasize that this is an opportunity for supervisors to gain insights into their employees' needs and to discuss how best to support and empower them.)
-Provide each supervisor with a discussion guide or sample questions, *such as follows*:
—"What challenges are you currently facing in your role?"
—"What tools or resources would help you feel more empowered in your work?"
—"Are there any skills you'd like to develop to improve your confidence or efficiency?"
—"How do you feel about the support you currently receive?
—How could it be improved?"
-Remind supervisors that the goal is to actively listen and collaboratively identify ways to address employees' needs.

2. One-on-One Needs Discussions (20-30 minutes per supervisor)
-Each supervisor meets individually with an employee to discuss their current needs. *Encourage supervisors to do the following:*
—Start with open-ended questions to allow employees to express their needs, challenges, and any suggestions they may have.
—Practice active listening, showing understanding through non-verbal cues, summarizing key points, and asking clarifying questions.
—Explore solutions collaboratively, asking employees for

STEP FIVE ACTIVITY

ideas on how their needs could be addressed and how the supervisor can best support them.
-Supervisors should take notes during each conversation to capture key insights and action items, while maintaining confidentiality where necessary.

3. Group Reflection and Sharing (20-30 minutes)
-After the one-on-one discussions, gather supervisors for a group debrief. *Discuss the following:*
—Common themes or needs that emerged from the conversations.
—Any unexpected insights or challenges encountered during the discussions.
—Initial ideas on how to address these needs or suggestions from employees.
-Invite supervisors to share any commitments they've made with their employees and any immediate actions they plan to take to support and empower them.

4. Identify Action Steps and Next Steps (10-15 minutes)
-Ask each supervisor to identify one or two immediate action steps they can take to address their employees' needs and support their empowerment. *Examples could include the following:*
—Providing access to training or development opportunities.
—Adjusting workflows or resources to meet specific challenges.
—Establishing regular check-ins to discuss progress and address ongoing needs.
-Encourage supervisors to follow up with each employee in a few weeks to review progress, discuss any improvements or adjustments, and ensure employees feel supported.

5. Wrap-Up and Accountability (5-10 minutes)
-Conclude by summarizing the importance of understanding and addressing employee needs. Emphasize that empowering

employees is an ongoing process that requires regular communication, follow-up, and adaptation.

-Set a follow-up meeting in the coming month for supervisors to discuss their progress, share any challenges, and celebrate successes.

Summary:
This activity builds open communication between supervisors and employees, helping supervisors to gain a deeper understanding of their teams' needs and empowering employees by addressing their specific challenges. Through these discussions, supervisors learn how to better support their teams, contributing to an environment where employees feel valued, capable, and motivated to excel in their roles.

STEP 6: EXPERIENCE

The sixth and final step of developing a solution-focused culture is experiencing success. For the purposes of this model, we have defined success as the achievement of meaningful progress toward organizational goals through innovation and problem-solving. True success is not only measured by outcomes, but by how effectively individuals and teams work together, overcome challenges, and apply their strengths to create lasting value. Every victory, no matter the size, contributes to the organization's ability to continually adapt and thrive. Success in a solution-focused culture is not only achievement, but recognition and reinforcement. It's not simply about reaching a goal and moving on, but understanding how each success is part of a larger journey that strengthens the organization and its people.

Achieving Success

In a solution-focused culture, achieving success is the responsibility of every employee. Success is a product of clear organizational goals, engaged teams, and empowered individuals working together toward a common purpose. It's about overcoming challenges, adapting to new circumstances, and con-sistently finding better solutions, in addition to the realization of the goal.

In the story of Clearview, we saw the culmination of the six steps in a solution-focused culture when the team met to solve the issues with three development applications. We saw a group made up of different departments embrace the idea of service and a solution-focused culture. They used the hurdles facing each development to work with the applicant to resolve issues and accomplish their desired goal. TJ's team found greater job satisfaction in helping the applicants not only meet the city's requirements but also reach a solution as close to the applicants' original plan as possible. By doing this, the team moved from finding purpose in regulation, to finding purpose in being a resource to the community. Success like this will look different in each application, but when the team sets aside a need to feel self-important or assert their power and replaces it with a desire to work collaboratively to solve problems, everyone involved will be more fulfilled.

Celebrating Success

As leaders, we often accomplish our goals and move on to the next one without taking time to reflect. This reflection, or celebration, is key for both leaders and employees. Celebrating successes strengthens a solution-focused culture. When employees feel their efforts are recognized, they become more engaged and committed to the organization's goals.

When using celebration as a tool, it is important to highlight the behaviors and mindsets that led to the achievement and the impact this achievement has on the organization and community. Public acknowledgment during team meetings is crucial for each participant to understand their role in the success of the project. For smaller-scale wins, personalized praise on the individual level can be just as motivating.

STEP 6: EXPERIENCE

The key is to connect these celebrations to the organization's core values, teamwork, innovation, or resilience, and highlight how those values were demonstrated throughout the process.

By intentionally celebrating successes, organizations not only create a positive feedback cycle but also make employees feel valued. This feeling of value will boost confidence and motivate them to strive for future achievements. Celebrations become moments of reflection and appreciation, where teams can pause to recognize their hard work before moving forward with renewed energy.

Strategies for celebrating organizational success include:

-Continuous feedback: Focus on what helped the project and how these behaviors can be continued. This helps teams to internalize the behaviors that contributed to success and fosters a mindset of ongoing improvement.

-Structured recognition programs: Highlight successful efforts that demonstrate alignment with the organization's core values. These structured programs offer scheduled opportunities to highlight successes and motivate others to work toward their goals.

-Share your story: Success stories should be relatable, relevant examples of how the team overcame challenges and contributed to achieving results. Sharing these experiences reinforces the solution-focused mindset and inspires others to take initiative.

By celebrating organizational success, you will teach employees to consistently apply the strategies that lead to success, building a foundation of confidence and capability. This reinforcement creates a culture where success is not just

STEP 6: EXPERIENCE

a momentary achievement but a continuous process of growth and excellence.

Celebrating success is essential for cultivating a solution-focused culture. Achievements highlight the organization's collective progress, while celebrations boost motivation and morale, embedding the lessons learned into ongoing practices. When success is embraced in this cyclical manner, it fosters a stronger, more engaged, and resilient culture, enabling the organization to tackle new challenges with confidence and creativity.

STEP SIX ACTIVITY

All-Staff Meeting

Objective:
To assess employee engagement levels, gather feedback on the organization's strengths and areas for improvement, and foster a positive work culture by celebrating the year's successes with all staff. This activity strengthens team morale, shows appreciation, and allows for meaningful employee input to shape future goals and initiatives.

Materials Needed:
-Digital or paper survey platform for anonymous responses
-Survey questions developed in collaboration with leadership and HR
-Presentation materials for the all-staff meeting (projector, slides, etc.)
-Food, drinks, and any awards or recognition items for the celebration meeting
-Prepared list of successes and achievements from the past year

STEP SIX ACTIVITY

Time Needed:
1-2 weeks to prepare and administer the survey
2-3 hours for the all-staff celebration meeting

Steps:
1. Develop and Distribute the Engagement Survey (3-4 weeks before the meeting)
-Collaborate with leadership and HR to create a set of questions that capture key aspects of employee engagement, such as job satisfaction, support from management, opportunities for growth, and alignment with organizational values.
-Ensure questions are clear, concise, and provide opportunities for both quantitative ratings and open-ended feedback.
-Administer the survey anonymously via an online platform (or on paper, if needed) and communicate the purpose of the survey to employees, emphasizing that their feedback will be used to improve the workplace.
-Provide a deadline for responses, generally 2-3 weeks, and send reminders as needed to encourage maximum participation.

2. Analyze and Summarize Survey Results
-After the survey closes, compile and analyze the data to identify key themes, trends, and areas for improvement.
—Focus on understanding both the positive feedback and constructive insights.
-Prepare a summary of the results, highlighting areas where employees feel supported and engaged as well as any recurring challenges or areas for growth.

3. Prepare for the All-Staff Meeting
-Create a presentation for the all-staff meeting that includes the following:
—A high-level overview of survey results (positive themes and key areas for improvement).

STEP SIX ACTIVITY

—Acknowledgment of the hard work and dedication employees have shown throughout the year.
—Highlights of the organization's major achievements and successes over the past year.
-Plan a celebration element, such as providing refreshments, recognizing outstanding contributions, or handing out awards for notable achievements.

4. Host the All-Staff Meeting and Present Survey Results (1-1.5 hours)
-Start the meeting by sharing the purpose of the session:
—Celebrate successes
—Acknowledge employee contributions
—Discuss insights from the engagement survey.
—Present a summary of the survey results.
—Focus on positive feedback first.
-Celebrate areas where employees feel engaged and appreciated.
-Discuss areas for improvement in a constructive, solution-oriented way.
-Outline any next steps or initiatives that leadership plans to take in response to the feedback.

5. Celebrate Year's Successes (30 minutes)
-Shift the focus to celebrating the year's accomplishments. Highlight specific achievements, projects, or milestones that have had a positive impact on the organization.
-Recognize employees or teams for their contributions, providing awards, certificates, or informal recognition for standout performance.
-Foster a celebratory atmosphere with food, music, or decorations to make employees feel appreciated.

STEP SIX ACTIVITY

6. Wrap-Up and Next Steps (5-10 minutes)
-Conclude the meeting by thanking everyone for their hard work and participation in the survey.
-Emphasize that the survey feedback will be used to improve the workplace and that leadership is committed to making progress on the identified areas.
-Encourage employees to continue sharing ideas and feedback throughout the year and highlight any ongoing or upcoming initiatives related to employee engagement.

Summary:
This activity boosts morale by celebrating employees' hard work and the organization's successes while demonstrating a commitment to continuous improvement. Sharing survey results and future plans shows employees that their voices are valued, promoting a sense of belonging and alignment with the organization's goals. The celebration fosters team spirit, gratitude, and motivation to continue striving for shared success in the year ahead.

A FINAL NOTE FROM THE AUTHORS

Thank you for joining us on the journey through *A Solution-Focused Culture*. This book is the product of many conversations about how to make government better, reflections, and real-world experiences from years of working within and alongside local government organizations. It is our sincere hope that TJ's journey resonates with you and inspires you to consider what's possible in your workplace.

Through this story, we aimed to illustrate how deeply impactful a shift in culture can be and how achievable it is—even for organizations facing bureaucracy, stagnation, or deeply ingrained habits. As we watched TJ and his team in Clearview work through challenges, develop a shared mission, and empower each other, we were reminded that transformation is always within reach if people are willing to work together toward a shared goal.

Creating a solution-focused culture in any organization requires a commitment to openness and innovation, and, most importantly, a willingness to truly listen to those who make up the organization. One of the most powerful lessons from TJ's journey was the importance of listening to the needs, frustrations, and insights of every team member, from top executives to the employees on the front lines. Each person's perspective adds depth to the culture and contributes to making it more dynamic and responsive. We understand that no two organizations are the same. Each organization, whether it's a government body, a nonprofit, or a corporation, has its own unique challenges and strengths. The steps and principles laid out in this book are designed to be adaptable, offering a foundational approach that can be shaped to meet the specific needs and circumstances of your team. We believe that by focusing on establishing a clear mission, aligning core values, and engaging employees at all levels, any organization can begin to create a culture where people are focused on solutions and empowered to make a difference.

However, it's crucial to recognize that building a solution-focused culture is not a "one and done" project. In our own experiences, we've seen that the most successful organizations are those that actively make time to review their culture, systems, and values. Culture is not static; it's always evolving as people join the team, as goals shift, and as the broader environment changes. Taking the time to check in on your organization's mission and values is a critical practice that keeps everyone moving in the same direction.

We encourage you to approach this journey with patience and persistence. Real change, as TJ and his team discovered, doesn't happen overnight. There will be setbacks, challenging moments, and perhaps even times when it feels like progress has stalled. But if you stay committed to the core principles outlined in this book, we're confident you'll begin to see the impact of a solution-focused approach within your team. Whether you're a seasoned leader, an HR professional, or a dedicated employee eager to make a difference, know that your role in this process is invaluable. Culture is shaped by each person within the organization, and the ripple effects of small, positive changes can be transformative. Every

A FINAL NOTE FROM THE AUTHORS

conversation you have, every decision you make, and every effort to understand a coworker or customer's perspective contributes to creating a workplace where people are seen, valued, and motivated to give their best.

Thank you for allowing us to share this vision with you. We hope that *A Solution-Focused Culture* serves as both a practical guide and a source of inspiration. As you embark on this journey in your own organization, we look forward to supporting you along the way. Please don't hesitate to reach out through our websites, **solution-focusedculture.com** and **tbspeaks.com**, for additional resources, tools, and guidance.

Here's to creating a future where every organization can become a place of innovation, collaboration, and purpose—one solution at a time.

With great appreciation,
Tim Bolduc & Jessica Leavins

Made in the USA
Columbia, SC
20 December 2024